NOTORIOUS RBG

NOTORIOUS
RBG

THE LIFE AND TIMES OF
RUTH BADER GINSBURG

IRIN CARMON & SHANA KNIZHNIK

DEY ST.
AN IMPRINT OF WILLIAM MORROW *PUBLISHERS*

HarperCollins books may be purchased for educational, business, or sales promotional use. For information please e-mail the Special Markets Department at SPsales@harpercollins.com.

FIRST EDITION

Designed by Katy Riegel and Shannon Nicole Plunkett
Hand lettering on chapter opening pages by Maria "Toofly" Castillo
Illustrations on pages 158–59 by Ping Zhu

Library of Congress Cataloging-in-Publication Data has been applied for.

ISBN 978-0-06-241583-7

20 OV/LSC 20 19

To the women on whose
shoulders we stand

CONTENTS

Authors' Note

HI, IT'S IRIN. A book is always a collaborative process, even when there is only one name on the cover. And this one has two, so I thought I'd introduce the two of us and tell you how we did it. Shana, then a law student, created the Notorious R.B.G. Tumblr as a digital tribute to Supreme Court Justice Ruth Bader Ginsburg, and she sparked an international phenomenon. I'm a journalist who interviewed RBG for MSNBC and will not try to wedge any more initials into this sentence. We are both #millennials who like the Internet but wanted to make something you could hold in your hands—or at least keep on your device for longer than a browser tab. We both researched and reported the book; I wrote it, so if you see "me," that's Irin. Shana also curated the images and fact-checked. We drew on RBG's own words, including my interview with her in February 2015, as well as our interviews with her family members, close friends, colleagues, and clerks. We also dug deep into RBG's archive at the Library of Congress. (You can skip to the end if you want to see her doodles during a conference in 1976.) We cite in the endnotes where we have gratefully relied on the reporting of others. Justice Ginsburg met with me in May 2015 to fact-check parts of the book, which involved both her patient generosity and my getting to text my boyfriend that a U.S. marshal was coming for him.

In homage to the Notorious B.I.G., the chapter titles in this book are inspired by his lyrics. We thank his estate and Sony Music for permission to use them. Artist Maria "TooFly" Castillo, who also runs a women's graffiti collective, beautifully rendered each chapter title. Throughout the book, you'll find photographs, some previously unpublished, and the work of artists and creators moved to show their love for RBG.

If you want to understand how an underestimated woman changed the world and is still out there doing the work, we got you. If you picked up this book only to learn how to get buff like an octogenarian who can do twenty push-ups, there's a chapter for you too. We even were lucky enough to wrangle some of the most brilliant legal minds out there to help us annotate key passages from RBG's legal writing.

RBG has been extraordinary all her life, but she never wanted to be a solo performer. She is committed to bringing up other women and underrepresented people, and to working together with her colleagues even when it seems impossible. We are frankly in awe of what we've learned about her, and we're pretty excited to share it with you.

1

NOTORIOUS

*"I just try to do the good job that I have to the best of my ability,
and I really don't think about whether I'm inspirational.
I just do the best I can."*

—RBG, 2015

THIS IS WHAT you should look for on this 90-degree June morning: The broadcast news interns pairing running shoes with their summer business casual, hovering by the Supreme Court's public information office. They're waiting to clamber down the marble steps of the court to hand off the opinions to an on-air correspondent. You should count the number of boxes the court officers lay out, because each box holds one or two printed opinions. Big opinions get their own box. This contorted ritual exists because no cameras are allowed inside the court. It jealously guards its traditions and fears grandstanding.

What happens inside the hushed chamber is pure theater. Below the friezes of Moses and Hammurabi, the buzz-cut U.S. marshals scowl the visitors into silence. The justices still have ceramic spittoons at their feet. At 10 A.M. sharp, wait for the buzzer and watch everyone snap to their feet. As a marshal cries "Oyez, oyez, oyez!" watch Associate Justice Ruth Bader Ginsburg, known around the court as RBG, as she takes her seat at the winged mahogany bench. Look around her neck. When the jabot with scalloped glass beads glitters flat against the top of RBG's black robe, it's bad news for liberals. That's her dissent collar.

On June 25, 2013, RBG's mirrored dissent collar glinted blue and yellow in reflected light. By then, in her ninth decade of life and her twentieth year on the court, RBG looked fragile and bowed, dwarfed by the black high-backed chair. But people who had counted her out when she had cancer were wrong, both times. People who thought she couldn't go on after the death of Marty Ginsburg, her husband of fifty-six years, were wrong too. RBG still showed up to do the work of the court without missing a day. She still pulled all-nighters, leaving her clerks voice mails with instructions at two or three in the morning.

The night before had been a long one. From RBG's perch, third from the right in order of seniority, she sometimes gazed up at the marble columns and wondered to herself if she was really there or if it were all a dream. But that Tuesday morning, her eyes were on her notes. The opinion was long finished, but she had something else to say, and she wanted to get it right. She scribbled intently as Justice Samuel Alito, seated to her left, read two opinions, about land and a bitter custody case involving Indian law. Those

Court artist sketch of Shelby County *dissent from the bench, June 25, 2013*

were not the cases the cameras were waiting for. It was a two-box day. There was one more left.

It was Chief Justice John Roberts's turn to announce an opinion he had assigned himself. The case was *Shelby County v. Holder*, a challenge to the constitutionality of a major portion of the Voting Rights Act.

Roberts has an amiable Midwestern affect and a knack for simple but elegant phrases that had served him well when he was a lawyer arguing before the justices. "Any racial discrimination in voting is too much," Roberts declared that morning. "But our country has changed in the last fifty years."

One of the most important pieces of civil rights legislation of the twentieth century had been born of violent images: the faces of murdered civil rights activists in Philadelphia, Mississippi; Alabama state troopers shattering the skull of young John Lewis on a bridge in Selma. But for this new challenge to voting rights that came from sixty miles from Selma, Roberts had a more comforting picture to offer the country. High black voter turnout had elected Barack Obama. There were black mayors in Alabama and Mississippi. The protections Congress had reauthorized only a few years earlier were no longer justifiable. Racism was pretty much over now, and everyone could just move on.

RBG waited quietly for her turn. Announcing a majority opinion in the court chamber is custom, but reading aloud in dissent is rare. It's like pulling the fire alarm, a public shaming of the majority that you want the world to hear. Only twenty-four hours earlier, RBG had sounded the alarm by reading *two* dissents from the bench, one in an affirmative action case and another for two workplace discrimination cases. As she had condemned "the court's disregard for the realities of the workplace," Alito, who had written the majority opinion, had rolled his eyes and shook his head. His behavior was unheard of disrespect at the court.

On the morning of the voting rights case, the woman Alito had replaced, RBG's close friend Sandra Day O'Connor, sat in the section reserved for VIPs. Roberts said his piece, then added, evenly, "Justice Ginsburg has filed a dissenting opinion."

RBG's voice had grown both raspier and fainter, but that morning there was no missing her passion. Alito sat frozen, holding his fist to his cheek. The noble purpose of the Voting Rights Act, RBG said, was to fight voter suppression that lingered, if more subtly. The court's conservative justices were supposed to care about restraint and defer to Congress, but they had wildly overstepped. "Hubris is a fit word for today's demolition of the VRA," RBG had written in her opinion. Killing the Voting Rights Act because it had worked too well, she had added, was like "throwing away your umbrella in a rainstorm because you are not getting wet."

At stake, RBG told the courtroom, was "what was once the subject of a dream, the equal citizenship stature of all in our polity, a voice to every voter in our democracy undiluted by race." It was an obvious reference to Martin

Luther King's famous "I Have a Dream" speech, but the phrase *equal citizen-ship stature* has special meaning to RBG in particular.

Forty years earlier, RBG had stood before a different set of justices and forced them to see that women were people too in the eyes of the Constitution. That women, along with men, deserved equal citizenship stature, to stand with all the rights and responsibilities that being a citizen meant. As part of a movement inspired by King's, RBG had gone from having doors slammed in her face to winning five out of six of the women's rights cases she argued before the Supreme Court. No one—not the firms and judges that had refused to hire a young mother, not the bosses who had forced her out of a job for getting pregnant or paid her less for being a woman—had ever expected her to be sitting up there at the court.

RBG often repeated her mother's advice that getting angry was a waste of your own time. Even more often, she shared her mother-in-law's counsel for marriage: that sometimes it helped to be a little deaf. Those words had served her in the bad old days of blatant sexism, through the conservative backlash of the eighties, and on a court of people essentially stuck together for life. But lately, RBG was tired of pretending not to hear. Roberts had arrived with promises of compromise, but a few short years and a handful of 5–4 decisions were swiftly threatening the progress for which she had fought so hard.

That 2012–2013 term, reading dissents from the bench in five cases, RBG broke a half-century-long record among all justices. Her dissent in the voting rights case was the last and the most furious. At nearly 10:30 A.M., RBG quoted Martin Luther King directly: "The arc of the moral universe is long, but it bends towards justice," she said. But then she added her own words: "if there is a steadfast commitment to see the task through to completion."

Not exactly poetry. But pure RBG. On or off the bench, she has always been steadfast, and when the work is justice, she has every intention to see it to the end. RBG has always been about doing the work.

People wondered where the quiet and seemingly meek RBG had gone, where this firebrand had come from. But the truth is, that woman had always been there.

YOU CAN'T SPELL
TRUTH WITHOUT RUTH

RBG had launched her protest from the bench on the morning of June 25 hoping people outside the court would listen. They did. As it sunk in that the court had, in the words of civil rights hero and Congressman John Lewis, put "a dagger in the heart of the Voting Rights Act," progressives felt a mix of despair and fury, but also admiration for how RBG had spoken up. "Everyone was angry on the Internet at the same time," remembers Aminatou Sow. Sow and her friend Frank Chi were both young, D.C.-

based digital strategists, used to channeling their frustrations into shareable objects. They wanted to do something. Chi spontaneously took a Simmie Knox painting of RBG, with its cool, watchful eyes and taut mouth, and gave it a red background and a crown inspired by the artist Jean-Michel Basquiat. Sow gave it words: "Can't spell truth without Ruth." They put it on Instagram, then plastered Washington with stickers.

In Cambridge, Massachusetts, twenty-six-year-old law student Hallie Jay Pope started drawing. Her comic showed RBG patiently explaining to her colleagues what had gone wrong in each case that week. "RBG" finally loses it with "Roberts's" glib exclamation in *Shelby*, "LOL racism is fixed!" Pope made an "I Heart RBG" shirt and donated the proceeds to a voting rights organization.

And in New York, twenty-four-year-old NYU law student Shana Knizhnik was aghast at the gutting of voting rights. The only bright spot for her was the unfettered rage of Justice Ginsburg—or, as her classmate Ankur Mandhania jokingly called the justice on Facebook, the Notorious R.B.G. Inspired, Shana took to Tumblr to create a tribute. To her, the reference to the 300-pound deceased rapper Notorious B.I.G. was both tongue-in-cheek and admiring. The humor was in the contrasts—the elite court and the streets, white and black, female and male, octogenarian and died too young. The woman who had never much wanted to make a stir and the man who had left his mark. There were similarities too. Brooklyn. Like the swaggering lyricist, this tiny Jewish grandmother who demanded patience as she spoke could also pack a verbal punch.

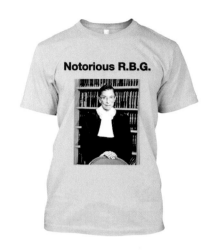

These appreciations were just the beginning. RBG, the woman once disdainfully referred to as "schoolmarmish," the wrong kind of feminist, "a dinosaur," insufficiently radical, a dull writer, is now a fond hashtag. Her every utterance is clickbait, and according to the headlines, she no longer says anything, but rather "eviscerates." At least two different Notorious R.B.G. signature cocktails can be drunk in two different cities. Turn on the Cartoon Network and you might glimpse an action figure named Wrath Hover Ginsbot ("appointed for life to kick your butt"). RBG's face is collaged, painted on fingernails, permanently tattooed on at least three arms, and emblazoned on Valentines and greeting cards with cute puns.

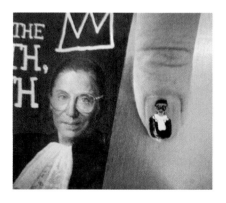

Hundreds of homemade RBG Halloween costumes come in baby and adult forms. By the spring of 2015, RBG was being namechecked anywhere a woman wanted to signal feminist smarts—by comedian Amy Schumer, by Lena Dunham on the show *Scandal,* and on *The Good Wife.* Comedian Kate McKinnon made RBG a recurring *Saturday Night Live*

character, who crows each zinger, "Ya just got Gins-burned!" and bumps to a hip-hop beat. "I just want to say that Ruth Bader Ginsburg is one of the most badass women in the world," Sow announces. "I think people who are no-nonsense people are rewarded greatly by the Internet."

All this is, to use the court's language, without precedent. No other justice, however scrutinized or respected, has so captured the public's imagination. The public image of RBG in her over thirty years as a judge was as a restrained moderate. The people closest to RBG find her entrance to the zeitgeist hilarious, if perplexing. "It's hard for me to think of someone less likely to care about being a cult figure," says David Schizer, a former RBG clerk and now a friend. "I would not have thought of her as hip," says her son, James. The adoring portrayal of an older woman like RBG as both fierce and knowing, points out the feminist author Rebecca Traister, is "a crucial expansion of the American imagination with regard to powerful women." For too long, Traister says, older women have been reduced in our cultural consciousness to "nanas, bubbes" or "ballbusters, nutcrackers, and bitches." RBG's old friend Gloria Steinem, who marvels at seeing the justice's image all over campuses, is happy to see RBG belie Steinem's own long-standing observation: "Women lose power with age, and men gain it."

Historically, one way women have lost power is by being nudged out the door to make room for someone else. Not long before pop culture discovered RBG, liberal law professors and commentators began telling her the best thing she could do for what she cared about was to quit, so that President Barack Obama could appoint a successor. RBG, ardently devoted to her job, has mostly brushed that dirt off her shoulder. Her refusal to meekly shuffle off the stage has been another public, high-stakes act of defiance.

Seniority determines many of the court's functions, from the order in which justices speak in meetings to who gets to assign opinions. When Justice John Paul Stevens retired in 2010, RBG became the most senior of the court's liberals, a leadership role she has embraced. RBG stays because she loves her work, but also, it seems, because she thinks the court is headed in an alarming direction. After years of toil, often in the shadows, she is poised to explain to the country just what is going wrong. "I sense a shift in her willingness to be a public figure," RBG's former American Civil Liberties Union colleague Burt Neuborne says. "Perhaps I am a little less tentative than I was when I was a new justice," RBG told *The New Republic* in 2014. "But what really changed was the composition of the Court." It was a polite way of saying the court had lurched to the right.

RBG has never been one to shrink from a challenge. People who think she is hanging on to this world by a thread underestimate her. RBG's main concession to hitting her late seventies was to give up waterskiing.

fear the frill.

NOT A BOMB THROWER,
BUT A BOMBSHELL ACHIEVER

Who is Ruth Bader Ginsburg? She takes her time, but nothing is lost on her. "She's not just deliberative as a matter of principle but as a matter of temperament," her friend the critic Leon Wieseltier has said. "A conversation with her is a special pleasure because there are no words that are not preceded by thoughts." She is wholly committed, above all, to the work of the court. Kathleen Peratis, who succeeded RBG as director of the Women's Rights Project at the ACLU, said years ago, "Ruth is almost pure work. The anecdote that describes her best is that there are no anecdotes." (The second part is not strictly true.) She has survived tragedies and calamities. People have found her somber, but it is sometimes because her humor is so deadpan dry that it escapes many. She can be exacting, but rewards with loyalty and generosity. She had a passionate love affair with her husband that lasted almost sixty years.

RBG is a woman who, to use another phrase that mattered a lot to her, defied stereotypes. When she was nominated to the Supreme Court, the *Washington Post* jointly interviewed two of her old ACLU colleagues, Peratis and former legal director Mel Wulf, and the pair struggled to explain RBG. "She's conventional socially and politically and in every way, except for her intellect," Wulf said, a tad dismissively. Peratis cut in, "Yeah, but Mel, you have to admit it was pretty unconventional in those days for a woman to raise a family, hold a job, go to law school." Wulf, a man of the 1960s, shrugged. "I'll say this, she is by no means a bomb thrower," he insisted.

"But," said Peratis, "the things she achieved were bombshells."

Put another way, RBG was already a radical just by being herself—a woman who beat the odds to make her mark. Early in her career, RBG wanted to work at a law firm, maybe teach a little. The world as it was had no room for her. That injustice left her no choice but to achieve bombshells. It was easy to miss, maybe because it didn't look like male bomb throwing. Or because she and her peers had transformed the world so much it was hard to remember, in retrospect and without living it, how hard it had been.

And yet as this book's closer look at her life and work shows, RBG is about more than simply breaking glass ceilings to join a man's world. As the cofounder of the Women's Rights Project at the ACLU, and often called the Thurgood Marshall of the women's rights movement, RBG devised careful, incremental plans for revolutionary goals. She imagined a world where men transformed themselves alongside women and where sexual and reproductive freedom was grounded in women's equality, and then she worked to make it real. Many of her ideals, from the liberation of men to the valuing of caregivers, remain unrealized. RBG's longtime friend Cynthia Fuchs Epstein says, "I think had she not had this persona as this very soft-spoken, neat, and tidy person, with a conventional life, she would have been considered a flaming radical."

If very few people recognized these things about RBG, she had preferred to keep it that way. "She subordinated her own persona into this machine," says Neuborne. "The star of every production she had was the law, not the lawyer."

But the arrival of two Bush appointees to the court gave a narrow majority to a conservative agenda of undermining remedies for racial justice, reproductive rights, access to health care, and protections for workers, while giving corporations ever more rights and political influence. Even the current balance, tipped rightward with a chance of wobble, is precarious. The next president may appoint as many as three justices.

RBG is determined to stick around and remind her colleagues and the country what she believes is America's unfinished promise. She likes to quote the opening words of the Constitution: "We the People of the United States, in order to form a more perfect Union." Beautiful, yes, but as she always points out, "we the people" originally left out a lot of people. "It would not include me," RBG said, or enslaved people, or Native Americans. Over the course of the centuries, people left out of the Constitution fought to have their humanity recognized by it. RBG sees that struggle as her life's work.

Maybe that's why she's keeping herself in fighting shape in the meantime. In late November 2014, RBG felt a little faint during a workout session with her regular personal trainer and had surgery so a stent could be placed in her right coronary. But she had plans to keep. RBG had invited Shana, Frank Chi, Aminatou Sow, and Ankur Mandhania to visit the court. "I would be glad to greet the clever creators of the Notorious R.B.G. in chambers," she wrote. On December 10, the morning of a two-hour oral argument about the Federal Tort Claims Act of 1946, the mememakers arrived.

At around noon, they filed tentatively into her chambers, as each justice's personal domain is known. RBG stood, flanked by her clerks. Her slender wrist was slightly bruised from the heart stent procedure. Her guests asked her what message she had for all the young people who admired her.

RBG paused to think it over. "You can tell them," she replied, "I'll be back doing push-ups next week."

Cheers,

Ruth Bader Ginsburg

2

BEEN IN THIS GAME
FOR YEARS

December 1853

"Was invited to sit in the Chief Justice's seat. As I took the place, I involuntarily exclaimed: 'Who knows, but this chair may one day be occupied by a woman.' The brethren laughed heartily."

—abolitionist feminist
Sarah Grimké

July 19–20, 1848

"We hold these truths to be self-evident: that all men and women are created equal."
—Declaration of Sentiments
at Seneca Falls

January 4, 1897: A woman abducted from her home at gunpoint wasn't raped, the Supreme Court says in *Mills v. United States,* because for an act to be rape, "more force is necessary."

| 1820 | 1830 | 1840 | 1850 | 1860 | 1870 | 1880 | 1890 | 1900 |

1828: Supreme Court justices bunk together, until one lady ruins it for everyone by insisting on living with her husband.

July 28, 1868: The Fourteenth Amendment to the Constitution, recognizing the citizenship rights of ex-slaves, promises equal protection under the law, but makes it clear only men's voting rights count.

April 15, 1873: The Supreme Court allows Illinois to block Myra Bradwell from practicing law just because she's a woman. In a 2011 reenactment of the case, RBG rules for Bradwell.

"The paramount destiny and mission of women are to fulfill the noble and benign offices of wife and mother. This is the law of the Creator."
—Justice Joseph P. Bradley, in a concurrence in *Bradwell v. Illinois*

"The method of communication between the Creator and the jurist is never disclosed."
—RBG, brief to the Supreme Court, 1972

"When you say you have 'no available graduates' whom you could recommend for appointment as my clerk, do you include women? It is possible I may decide to take one, if I can find one who is absolutely first-rate."
—Justice William O. Douglas, 1944

August 18, 1920: The Nineteenth Amendment recognizes women's right to vote, though violent barriers remain for women of color.

June 10, 1932: Martin D. Ginsburg, future husband of RBG, is born.

1944: Lucille Lomen becomes the first female clerk at the Supreme Court.

1900 **1910** **1920** **1930**

1903: Celia Amster, RBG's mother, is born.

March 15, 1933: Joan Ruth Bader, nicknamed Kiki, is born in Brooklyn.

June 1950: Celia Bader dies one day before her daughter's high school graduation.

Fall 1950: RBG enrolls at Cornell.

May 17, 1954: In *Brown v. Board of Education of Topeka,* the Supreme Court reverses itself on "separate but equal."

June 1954: Ruth Bader graduates from Cornell. She marries Marty at his family's home.

July 21, 1955: Jane Ginsburg is born.

November 20, 1961: The Supreme Court signs off on making jury service optional because "woman is still regarded as the center of home and family life."

"NOT GUILTY!"—ON ACCOUNT OF HIS GOOD LOOKS

December 1962: Civil rights activist Pauli Murray proposes using the Fourteenth Amendment to argue against sexist laws.

1940   **1950**   **1960**

1953: Simone de Beauvoir's *The Second Sex* is published in the United States.

1956: RBG enrolls in Harvard Law School, one of only nine women in her class. In her second year, Marty is diagnosed with cancer.

"The study of law was unusual for women of my generation. For most girls growing up in the 1940s, the most important degree was not your B.A., but your M.R.S."
—RBG

1958: Marty graduates from Harvard Law School. RBG transfers to Columbia University School of Law.

1959: RBG graduates from Columbia Law at the top of her class but can barely get a job.

1963: RBG becomes the second woman to teach full-time at Rutgers School of Law.

RUTH B. GINSBURG
Assistant Professor of Law
B.A. Cornell Univ.
LL.B. Columbia Univ.

"[The dean explained] it was only fair to pay me modestly, because my husband had a very good job."
—RBG

June 10, 1963: President John F. Kennedy signs the Equal Pay Act, which bans discrimination in pay on the basis of sex. It's full of loopholes.

June 7, 1965: The Supreme Court finds that Connecticut's birth control ban violates a "right to marital privacy."

June 13, 1967: President Johnson nominates famed civil rights litigator Thurgood Marshall (and RBG inspiration) to be the first black justice of the Supreme Court.

1960

September 8, 1965: RBG's son, James Ginsburg, is born.

July 2, 1964: President Lyndon Johnson signs into law the Civil Rights Act, which contains a last-minute ban on sex discrimination in employment.

Spring 1970: RBG teaches her first class on women and the law.

1965: RBG publishes her first book, *Civil Procedure in Sweden,* with Anders Bruzelius.

"That's why when the Supreme Court faces a tricky question of Swedish civil procedure, we always go straight to Justice Ginsburg."
—Justice Elena Kagan

"Unless [sex discrimination is banned], the white women of this country would be drastically discriminated against in favor of a Negro woman."
—Representative Glenn Andrews of Alabama

*"The Department of Justice, I am sure, doesn't have any male secretaries. . . .
They hire women secretaries because they are better."*

—Chief Justice Warren Burger at oral argument for *Phillips v. Martin-Marietta*,
December 9, 1970

June 25, 1971: RBG writes her first brief to the Supreme Court in *Reed v. Reed*.

January 1972: RBG becomes the first female tenured professor at Columbia Law School.

June 23, 1972: Richard Nixon signs into law Title IX, which bans sex discrimination in education.

1974: RBG publishes the first-ever casebook on sex discrimination. She insists that the authors' names be listed alphabetically, even though doing so means the one man's name will come first.

CONSTITUTIONAL ASPECTS OF
SEX-BASED DISCRIMINATION

1970

1980

Spring 1972: RBG cofounds the Women's Rights Project at the American Civil Liberties Union.

January 22, 1973: In *Roe v. Wade* and *Doe v. Bolton,* the Supreme Court makes abortion legal throughout the United States. RBG is uneasy about how the court got there, and how fast.

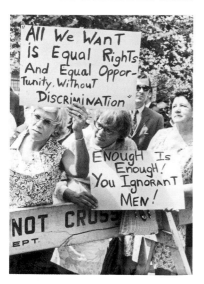

*"This right of privacy . . . is broad enough to encompass a
woman's decision whether or not to terminate her pregnancy."*
—Justice Harry Blackmun, *Roe v. Wade*

April 11, 1980: President Jimmy Carter nominates RBG to the United States Court of Appeals for the District of Columbia Circuit.

May 13, 1994: President Clinton nominates Stephen Breyer to replace Harry Blackmun as associate justice.

June 26, 1996: RBG writes the majority opinion in the landmark case *United States v. Virginia,* requiring the Virginia Military Institute to admit women.

June 14, 1993: President Bill Clinton nominates RBG to be an associate justice of the United States Supreme Court.

1980

1990

August 19, 1981: President Ronald Reagan nominates Sandra Day O'Connor to be the first woman on the Supreme Court. Male justices who had made noises over the years about resigning if a woman ever joined their ranks stay put.

Summer 1999: RBG is diagnosed with colorectal cancer. She does not miss a day on the bench.

December 12, 2000: RBG is one of four dissenters in *Bush v. Gore,* which effectively declares George W. Bush president.

"The wisdom of the court's decision to intervene and the wisdom of its ultimate determination await history's judgment."

—RBG, *Bush v. Gore* dissent

July 1, 2005: Sandra Day O'Connor announces her retirement. President George W. Bush nominates D.C. Circuit judge John Roberts as her replacement.

"To my sorrow, I am now what [O'Connor] was her first twelve years on the court—the lone woman."
—RBG

September 2005: Chief Justice Rehnquist, whom RBG would continue to call "my chief," dies. President Bush switches Roberts's nomination to chief justice and nominates Appeals Court Judge Samuel Alito to replace O'Connor.

May 26, 2009: President Obama nominates Federal Appeals Court Judge Sonia Sotomayor to the Supreme Court. She is the first Latina justice.

May 29, 2007: RBG reads her dissent from the bench in the sex discrimination case of Lilly Ledbetter.

"I like the idea that we're all over the bench. It says women are here to stay."
—RBG

2000

2010

April 18, 2007: RBG launches her era of furious dissent with the abortion case *Gonzales v. Carhart.*

"The Court . . . pretends that its decision protects women."
—RBG, summarizing her dissent from the bench

February 5, 2009: RBG has surgery to remove a cancerous tumor.

February 23, 2009: RBG is back on the bench.

February 24, 2009: RBG attends President Obama's first speech to Congress.

November 4, 2008: Barack Obama is elected the first black president.

"I don't know. I hear that Justice Ginsburg has been working on her jump shot."
—Barack Obama, after being invited to play basketball at the nation's highest court

"I wanted people to see that the Supreme Court isn't all male."
—RBG

March 27, 2013

"There's full marriage and then there's sort of skim milk marriage."
—RBG at oral argument in *United States v. Windsor*,
the successful challenge to the Defense of Marriage Act

June 27, 2010: Marty Ginsburg dies after complications from metastatic cancer.

June 25, 2013: As RBG dissents in a case gutting the Voting Rights Act, Notorious R.B.G., the Tumblr, is born.

June 30, 2014: In *Burwell v. Hobby Lobby,* the Supreme Court allows corporations to refuse contraceptive coverage to women based on the employer's religious belief.

2010

2020

May 10, 2010: President Obama nominates Solicitor General Elena Kagan to the Supreme Court.

August 2013: RBG becomes the first Supreme Court justice to officiate a same-sex wedding.

February 28, 2015: RBG becomes a recurring character on *Saturday Night Live*'s Weekend Update, issuing "Ginsburns" between dance moves.

February 12, 2015: RBG admits she was not "100 percent sober" at the State of the Union.

"I think it will be one more statement that people who love each other and want to live together should be able to enjoy the blessings and the strife in the marriage relationship."
—RBG on performing same-sex weddings

> "The court, I fear, has ventured into a minefield."
>
> —RBG, *Hobby Lobby* dissent

3

I GOT A
STORY to TELL

"I feel like a very lucky girl who grew up in Brooklyn."

—RBG, 1996

THE YEARBOOK for James Madison High School's class of 1950 predicted that one senior would be a Supreme Court justice. As of this writing, Joel Sheinbaum is still practicing dentistry on Long Island. There was no particular prediction for Ruth Bader, nicknamed Kiki by her older sister. Having made it to the relative idyll of Brooklyn, the Jewish parents of Flatbush longed to say "my son the doctor, the lawyer," as Richard Salzman, Kiki's classmate, remembered. "The girls were supposed to marry doctors or lawyers."

The yearbook entry for Ruth Bader shows a photo of a sweet-faced girl with bobbed hair. It notes that she was a cellist, that she twirled the baton (but not that she chipped her tooth once doing so), that she was in the honor society and treasurer of the Go-Getters club. People remembered her as popular but quiet. "She ran with a group of girls who were not very tall and chatted and seemed to have a good time," recalls another classmate, Hesh Kaplan. In summers at Camp Che-Na-Wah in the Adirondacks, Kiki acquired the title of camp rabbi and met a nice boy who was bound for law school.

In those days, some of the Irish, Italian, and Polish parents still thought there was a chance Jewish kids would make matzohs of their children's blood. Fights broke out in alleyways over Jews killing Christ. Kiki remembered a sign at a bed-and-breakfast in Pennsylvania: NO DOGS OR JEWS ALLOWED. But Brooklyn was a nice place to grow up. When Kiki got too old to be read to, her mother would drop her off at the library once a week and go get her hair done while Kiki picked her five books of the week. For a while, her favorites were books about Greek and Norse mythology, and then she graduated to Nancy

RUTH BADER
1584 East 9th Street
Arista, Treas. of Go-Getters, School
Orchestra, Twirlers, Sec. to English
Department Chairman, Feature Ed-
itor Term Newspaper
Cornell University

Drew. "This was a girl who was an adventurer, who could think for herself, who was the dominant person in her relationship with her young boyfriend," RBG remembered happily. Because the library was one floor above a Chinese restaurant, "I learned to love the smell of Chinese food in those days."

The Catholics went to parochial school, the Jews to Madison. There wasn't much about Kiki that seemed different from the other kids. They rode their bikes to and from school. Their parents tried to forget what had happened in Europe. They listened to the radio show and then watched the television version of *The Goldbergs,* with a Jewish mother who shouted out of windows like theirs sometimes did. They talked uneasily about Judy Coplon, the Madison graduate who was arrested for spying for the Soviets in Kiki's junior year, and wondered if this time the government was going after the Jews.

What was different about Kiki was that she lived in a house that had the smell of death, as she later called it. She told no one her mother had been slowly dying of cervical cancer since Kiki was thirteen, or that her sister, Marilyn, had died of meningitis when Kiki was two. But it was her secret to keep. She didn't want anyone feeling sorry for her. That same year, she turned thirteen, and Kiki's friends gathered over tobacco smoke and teased her that she wouldn't take a puff because she was scared of choking. Cigarettes were disgusting, she thought, but she would have no one thinking she was afraid. (Her smoking habit lasted about forty years.)

When her mother got very sick, Kiki tried to think about what would make her mother happy and settled on doing her homework by her mother's bed. She would not forget the time she had brought to her mother a less-than-perfect report card. That was the end of imperfect report cards.

Celia Amster was born in New York four months after her family fled the Austro-Hungarian Empire. She was the fourth of seven children, and at fifteen, she easily graduated from high school with top grades. Celia's parents had big dreams—for her eldest brother. Each week, a chunk of Celia's earnings from working as a bookkeeper in Manhattan's garment district went to her brother's tuition at Cornell. When Celia married Nathan Bader, whose family had left a shtetl near pogrom-ravaged Odessa, and who had learned English in night school, that was the end of Celia working for money. It wouldn't do for a woman to keep working. People would think her husband couldn't support her, even if that was almost true when her husband's trade was fur during the Depression and he'd never had much of a knack for business. Celia did help out a bit with the bookkeeping. Even as a young girl, Kiki could feel the sharpness of her mother's disappointment. Celia Amster Bader, her daughter would often say as an adult, was perhaps the most intelligent person she ever knew.

Fifteen-year-old RBG as camp rabbi at Che-Na-Wah in the Adirondacks

By the end of high school, Kiki had not disappointed her mother. She'd gotten into Cornell, and her name was all over the high school graduation roster. Ruth Bader, English Scholarship Medal. Ruth Bader, New York State scholarship. Ruth Bader, slated to speak as part of the Round Table Forum of Honor. But Kiki never made it to graduation. On the day before the ceremony, her mother died.

As the house on East Ninth Street filled with mourning women, Kiki watched dully, because no woman counted for the minyan, the quorum of adults needed for a prayer under Jewish law. Kiki herself did not count. At Passover seder, Kiki loved to ask the most questions, but no girls were allowed to join the boys studying for their bar mitzvahs. When Celia's mourners left and Nathan's business suffered without her disciplined eye, Nathan had to cut his donations to Temple Beth El. The family was banished to the annex. Jewish law taught Kiki about a commitment to justice, but after her mother died, it took her a long time to see herself in the faith.

Celia's instructions would remain carved in her daughter's memory. Ruth was to always be a lady. "That meant always conduct yourself civilly, don't let emotions like anger or envy get in your way," RBG later explained. "Hold fast to your convictions and your self-respect, be a good teacher, but don't snap back in anger. Anger, resentment, indulgence in recriminations waste time and sap energy." Few mothers of that time gave their daughters Celia's second piece of advice: Always be independent.

This was a practical as well as philosophical admonition. After her mother's death, Kiki learned Celia had quietly scraped together eight thousand dollars for her daughter's education. Haunted by the Depression, when she had learned to never buy anything on credit, Celia had spread her savings across five banks with no more than two thousand dollars in each account. "It was one of the most trying times in my life, but I knew that she wanted me to study hard and get good grades and succeed in life," RBG said later. "So that's what I did."

YOU COULD DROP A BOMB OVER HER HEAD

Not long after she had arrived in Ithaca, New York, in the fall of 1950, Kiki created a mental map of every women's bathroom on the Cornell campus. The one in the architecture school was best. That's where she would smuggle books, going into a stall until her coursework was done. There were four men to every woman, and parents and daughters said aloud what a good place it was to find a man. Thanks to the competition for the spots reserved for women, RBG remembered, "The women were a heck of a lot smarter than the men." But they hid their smarts.

Kiki was hiding too. Mostly from the parties. No one, male or female, wanted to look serious, but she couldn't hide her intensity. "You could drop a bomb over her head and she wouldn't know it," says Anita Fial, a high school classmate and her Cornell suitemate. Seven Jewish girls who had come from big cities lived along a corridor in Clara Dickson Hall and called themselves KLABHIJ, for each of their initials. Kiki came first. After dinner on weeknights, the girls had to be indoors for the 10 P.M. curfew, ready for check-in. Girls had to live on campus, but boys were allowed to live in apartments in Ithaca, coming and going as they pleased. After curfew, the other girls of KLABHIJ played bridge on the floor but Kiki would just keep working.

RBG

The Alpha Epsilon Phi sorority at Cornell in 1953

Celia had wanted her daughter to be a teacher, a solid job for a woman. Kiki tried, and then dropped, student teaching. She preferred her European literature class with Vladimir Nabokov, then an unknown émigré who taught her to think carefully where each word should go. She chose government as her major and took an undergraduate class in constitutional law from the legendary professor Robert E. Cushman. Kiki had begun to notice things about the country in which she had felt lucky to have been born. World War II, which she later called "a war against racism," had ended only five years before. "I came to understand that our troops in that war were separated by race, until the end. So there was something wrong about that," she said.

There was something wrong with what happened her senior year too. Marcus Singer, a professor of zoology at Cornell, was hauled before Senator Joseph McCarthy's Permanent Subcommittee on Investigations and indicted for refusing to name fellow members of a Marxist study group. When Cornell stripped Singer of his teaching duties, the campus was in an uproar. Kiki was aghast. She'd begun working as a research assistant to Professor Cushman, helping him put together an exhibition on book burning, and here was censorship unfolding before her eyes. Cushman pointed out that lawyers had come to Singer's rescue. "I got the idea that being a lawyer was a pretty good thing," RBG recalled, "because in addition to practicing a profession, you could do something good for your society."

Her father, Nathan, worried about Kiki wanting to be a lawyer. So few women had made it. How would she support herself? He had reason to relent by the time she was a senior. His Kiki had, by then, found a good man to support her. She herself did not see it that way. Kiki was just happy that Marty Ginsburg, one year ahead of her at Cornell, was the first boy she ever met who cared that she had a brain.

They had started out as good friends. Irma, the I in KLABHIJ, had a boyfriend who knew the famously wisecracking Marty. Marty had a girlfriend at Smith, and Kiki's boyfriend from Camp Che-Na-Wah went to Columbia Law School, so she saw him on weekends at best. Irma and her boyfriend thought introducing the two might mean the foursome could head to town in Marty's gray Chevy. Freed of the pressures of courting, Marty told Kiki everything on his mind. It was a good way to start a romantic relationship, which is what it became. "There was a long, cold week at Cornell," RBG recalled. "So that's how we started. It occurred to me that Martin D. Ginsburg was ever so much smarter than my boyfriend at Columbia Law School." Marty made up his mind much faster. "I have no doubt that in our case I liked her more first," he recalled.

Marty moved through the world with an easy confidence, tempered by an impish sense of humor. "Ruth was a wonderful student and a beautiful young woman. Most of the men were in awe of her, but Marty was not," Carr Ferguson, a Cornell classmate and one of Marty's closest friends, remembered. "He's never been in awe of anybody. He wooed and won her by convincing her how much he respected her."

Where Kiki was shy and contained, Marty was the life of the party. His father, Morris, had risen through the garment industry to become vice president of Federated Department Stores; his mother, Evelyn, was an operagoer who quickly took her son's motherless girlfriend under her wing. Kiki became a regular at the Ginsburg home on Long Island. She worked one summer at A&S, one of Federated's stores, and on those suburban streets, she failed her driving test five times before passing the sixth.

Just because Evelyn didn't work outside the home didn't mean Marty expected the same from his future wife. He wanted them to marry and keep on working together, at Harvard. His idea was, Marty later recalled, "to be in the same discipline so there would be something you could talk about, bounce ideas off of, know what each other was doing, and we actually sat down and by process of elimination came up with the law." Marty had dropped his chemistry major because it interfered with golf practice, so medical school was out. Harvard Business School didn't accept women. So they settled on law. "I have thought deep in my heart," Marty would confess forty years later, "that Ruth always intended that to be the case."

They both made it into Harvard Law School. Marty, a year older, enrolled immediately while Kiki stayed in Ithaca to finish at Cornell. In June 1954, they married in the Ginsburgs' living room, just days after Kiki's graduation from Cornell. There were eighteen people present, because in Judaism that number symbolizes life. Moments before the ceremony, as Kiki made last-minute arrangements, Evelyn asked her to come with her to the bedroom.

The newlyweds at Fort Sill, Oklahoma, in fall 1954

"Dear," said Evelyn, whom Kiki would soon call Mother, "I'm going to tell you the secret of a happy marriage: It helps sometimes to be a little deaf." In her outstretched hand were a pair of earplugs.

It took some time for RBG to understand what Evelyn was trying to tell her. During the honeymoon in Europe, her first time outside of the country, it became clear. "My mother-in-law meant simply this," RBG said. "Sometimes people say unkind or thoughtless things, and when they do, it is best to be a little hard of hearing—to tune out and not snap back in anger or impatience."

Cambridge would have to wait a little longer for the Ginsburgs. The U.S. Army had other plans for Marty, who had been in the Reserve Officers' Training Corps in college. They were headed to Oklahoma for two years to live at the Fort Sill base.

While Marty found he liked teaching at Fort Sill's artillery school—he had been good at golf, and was good at shooting—RBG struggled. She worked at a law firm but couldn't type to save her life, so she took the civil service exam to work for the federal government. Workers were classified according to a "general schedule," or GS, of earnings and responsibility; as a GS-5, RBG qualified to be a claims adjuster. Then she innocently mentioned at the Social Security office that employed her that she was three months pregnant. Well, then, she was told, she couldn't possibly go to Baltimore for training. Her rank promptly dropped to GS-2, the lowest: less money, less responsibility. Another army wife in the office with a GS-5 rank was pregnant too, RBG learned, but told no one until she had to. That woman went to Baltimore. But she was also expected to quit before she gave birth.

Seeing the unfairness of petty bureaucracy and how it fell harder on some people's shoulders than others, RBG began bending the rules, just a little. Week after week, she saw the same weathered faces coming in to try to register for Social Security, only to be sent back to look for the right papers. These visitors had no birth certificates, because when Native Americans had been born, no one official thought their births were worth recording. RBG silently decided that if someone looked sixty-five, a hunting or fishing license would do.

After two years in Oklahoma, RBG had to earn readmission to Harvard, and she got it. That was the easy part. Being a young mother on an army base had been surprisingly manageable. The officers' nursery started taking babies at two months and was open until midnight. But how could she handle law school as the mother of a toddler?

Evelyn had often comforted her, but this time it was Morris's words that shook her out of her panic. "Ruth, if you don't want to go to law school, you have the best reason in the world and no one would think less of you," Morris said. "But if you really want to go to law school, you will stop feeling sorry for yourself. You will find a way."

Ruth really wanted to go to law school.

SOMETHING STRANGE AND SINGULAR

On a fall evening in 1956, Ruth Bader Ginsburg was happy to have something to do with her hands. She had made it through a stiff dinner at Harvard Law School dean Erwin Griswold's house, and now wondered how long they would make small talk in a semicircle in Griswold's living room.

Each of the nine female students—all of the female students of their Harvard Law School class—had been paired with a professor. RBG shared an ashtray with the famous professor Herbert Wechsler. Forty years later, she would use uncharacteristically florid language to describe Wechsler: "He seemed to me then, as he has ever since, to combine the power and beauty of the Greek gods Zeus and Apollo." Wechsler was a chain smoker.

RBG anxiously tapped out the ash. Soon she could go home to Marty and their daughter, Jane, who had turned one in July. But Griswold wasn't ready to end the night. He wanted to savor the fact that he had, in his own telling, gotten women into Harvard Law School only six years earlier. RBG had just been relieved to see that Harvard was a place where women didn't hide their smarts.

Before he let them go, Griswold had a question. How, he asked, could each of these female students justify taking the place of a man?

As the students reddened and shifted, RBG wanted to crawl under the couch. She had none of the sass of Flora Schnall, who coolly replied that she thought Harvard Law School would be a good place to find a husband. After all, once you subtracted Marty Ginsburg's wife, there were eight Harvard Law women and around five hundred men. Then it was RBG's turn. As she jerked to her feet to answer, the ashtray slid from her lap to the floor, scattering ashes on the carpet. No one moved. Griswold waited.

"I wanted to know more about what my husband does," she mumbled. "So that I can be a sympathetic and understanding wife."

If Griswold knew she was lying, he didn't let on.

A faculty member later explained that it couldn't be true that women were discriminated against at Harvard Law School. "We try to take people who have something unusual, something different about them," he said. "If you're a bull fiddle player, for example, you would get a plus, and if you're a woman, you would get a plus." RBG was left feeling like she and the other women were exotic animals in a menagerie. They were, as she later put it, "something strange and singular."

Every time she thought she could just do her work, RBG was reminded again that she didn't belong there. "You felt in class as if all eyes were on you and that if you didn't perform well, you would be failing not only for yourself, but for all women," RBG remembered. Some professors held Ladies' Day, when they would call only on women, with humiliating questions.

RBG made the Law Review, a distinction Marty hadn't managed. She was one of two women—"roses amid the thorns," as a photographer put it while positioning them on either side of the men of the Law Review. One night, near midnight, she found herself frantic inside Lamont Library, barred from checking a citation because no women were allowed in that reading room. RBG begged the guard to let her stand at the door while he grabbed the journal for her, but he wouldn't budge. The annual banquet was a perk of being on the Law Review, but RBG wasn't allowed to bring her beloved mother-in-law to it, and the men weren't allowed to take their wives, because even though there were female members, it was still a boys' club. Women were

RBG

The men (and two women) of the Harvard Law Review, *1957/58*

barred from living in the dorms, the exact opposite policy from Cornell, and neither rule made sense to RBG. There was no women's bathroom in the main building, where exams were held. After that first year, a classmate named Rhoda Isselbacher, who was pregnant during the exam period, informed the men she would use their bathroom whether they liked it or not.

RBG didn't think to complain. She was lucky, in a way. Harvard had said she had to submit her husband's father's financials now that she was married, so her father-in-law, Morris, had agreed to pay her tuition. Some of her classmates worried that going to law school would ruin their chances of marriage, or that their husbands would tire of having wives with plans, but RBG had a husband who bragged that his wife had done better than him. He teased her only about her driving, and even RBG admitted she was a terrible driver.

By their second year in Cambridge, in 1957, RBG had worked out a kind of rhythm. Classes and studying until 4 P.M., then home to relieve the babysitter, a New England grandmotherly type.

Her hours with Jane before bed helped leaven the library time. Marty was realizing his lifelong passion for the tax code. Then the doctor found the tumor in his testicle. Cancer, which had already stolen RBG's mother, threatened to take Marty too. The doctor prescribed radical surgery and daily radiation for six weeks. The prognosis was grim.

The last thing RBG was going to do was to act like Marty was dying. So she threw everything into making sure he stayed on track in his studies, despite having missed all but two weeks of the semester. Who were the best note takers in his classes? She

Marty, Jane, and RBG in summer 1958

handed them carbon paper and told them to pass on the class notes. Each night, she typed these notes up, with the occasional help of a girlfriend of Marty's classmate.

Marty was weak, but he came alive when his classmates came by and they could argue the finer points of corporate reorganization. Sometimes he woke at midnight, and that was the only time he could eat. Too ill to type, he would lie on the couch and dictate to his wife his paper on loss corporations. When Marty fell asleep around 2 A.M., RBG would begin her own work. That was how she learned she could get by on just one or two hours of sleep, as long as she could sleep in a little on weekends.

Unable to think about a reality in which Marty had no future, RBG went to Dean Griswold and asked him if Marty's class standing could be based on his first two years. He would get whatever his grades would show, Griswold told her, and they would record that he had been sick. RBG went home and told her husband, "Do whatever you can do to pass. Only your first and second years will count." Asked sixty years later if this had been a white lie, RBG only said, "He was at ease for those exams."

Marty made it through, against all odds, and graduated. He even found work as a tax attorney at a firm in New York. The young family was determined to stay together, and RBG found herself again at Dean Griswold's mercy. She had waited so long for her Harvard degree. If she took her third-year classes at Columbia in New York, could she still get one? They didn't know how long Marty would live—couldn't they get a hardship exemption to the transfer policy? Again, Griswold refused.

RBG showed up on the Columbia campus too afraid to even ask whether the law school would grant her a degree. The handful of women at Columbia Law School didn't have it easy either. Hazel Gerber, whose son would one day be one of RBG's favorite clerks, once began a sentence in class with "I feel—" and her law professor cut in, "Miss Gerber: Women feel, men think." RBG's reputation preceded her. "We had heard that the smartest person on the East Coast was going to transfer, and that we were all going to drop down one rank," classmate Nina Appel later told the *New York Times*. They

were right to worry. RBG made the Law Review a second time and graduated tied for first in her class.

Harvard Law's strict transfer rules stayed in place for decades. In the
late seventies, as the policy came up for fresh scrutiny, Marty wrote a letter
to the *Harvard Law Record* to complain of his family's ordeal. The editors
published his letter, appending a note:

> *As Mr. Ginsburg told us, the Ruth in the letter is Ruth Bader
> Ginsburg, professor of law at Columbia and general counsel
> of the American Civil Liberties Union. Just think what else
> she might have accomplished had she enjoyed the benefits of a
> Harvard degree.*

LADY IS A
FOUR-LETTER WORD

One day in the 1959 term, Associate Justice Felix Frankfurter burst into
his chambers and announced to his clerks that he had unbelievable news.
Frankfurter held what was sometimes called the Jewish seat on the Supreme
Court. He had a habit of having Harvard Law professors pick his clerks. The
young men who served as Supreme Court law clerks—and they had almost
always been men—had the most elite entry-level jobs in the business, working closely with the justices to research and draft their opinions. The boys
would never guess who Professor Al Sacks wanted to send Frankfurter that
year, he told them: Ruth Bader Ginsburg.

Paul Bender, a Frankfurter clerk who had known RBG since James
Madison High School and through Harvard Law, ventured his support.
Frankfurter protested that Ginsburg "had a couple of kids, and her hus-
band has been ill, and you know that I work you guys very very hard, and I
do curse sometimes." Almost all of that was false. RBG had only one kid.
Bender believed he and his compatriots had "the softest job of all the law

clerks at the court." There was more shading of the truth, Bender said: "The justice did not use four-letter words." (There is no remaining evidence that, as a much retold story has it, Frankfurter demanded to know if RBG wore pants, as he despised girls who wore pants.)

Frankfurter had never refused a recommended candidate, but when word reached RBG that she would not clerk on the Supreme Court, she was not surprised. She knew that Judge Learned Hand, a Federal Court of Appeals judge she idolized, had a policy against hiring women because he was (actually) known to be potty-mouthed and didn't want to have to watch his language around women. She had gotten used to seeing sign-up sheets at Columbia for firm interviews that were labeled "men only." RBG had worked at the law firm of Paul Weiss one summer, but it turned out the firm had already hired one woman that year, and one was enough for them. (They hired Pauli Murray, a black woman whose work would one day have an enormous impact on RBG.) To her two interviews, RBG wore a black tailored suit that her mother-in-law had chosen for her. She got no offers. As RBG saw it, she had three strikes against her: She was a woman, the mother of a four-year-old, and a Jew.

Gerald Gunther, a constitutional law professor at Columbia, was determined to find his brilliant student a spot—even if it involved blackmail. Federal judge Edmund L. Palmieri of the Southern District of New York, a Columbia grad, always took Gunther's recommendation without question. But Palmieri was skeptical of Gunther's pick that year. Would RBG really be up to the job with a small child at home? Gunther promised that if it didn't work out, he would supply Palmieri with a male replacement. And if Palmieri didn't give this young lady a chance, Gunther swore he would never send Palmieri another clerk again. Whether carrot or stick, something worked.

Palmieri did not send the young Mrs. Ginsburg home. She worked even harder than she probably needed to, coming in on weekends and taking work home. Palmieri later said she was one of his best clerks ever. As it happened, Judges Hand and Palmieri lived around the corner from each other, and Palmieri often gave both Hand and Ginsburg a ride home from the federal courthouse. "The man would say or sing anything that came into his head," RBG remembered of Hand. "I once asked, 'Judge Hand, in this car you speak freely—you say words my mother never taught me. I don't seem to be inhibiting you.' He replied, 'Young lady, I'm not looking at you.'"

After she spent two years clerking, when the doors of corporate law firms tentatively swung open, RBG no longer wanted to walk through them. Instead, in 1961, she accepted an invitation for lunch at the Harvard Club with Hans Smit, a Dutchman she had met at Columbia. A few minutes after she'd entered from a small, red side door where the club begrudgingly let women in, Smit said, "Ruth, how would you like to coauthor a book about civil procedure in Sweden?" He was putting together a comparative law project at Columbia. Smit had no trouble finding men to go to France and Italy, but finding someone ready to become fluent in Swedish and then travel to Sweden to study the legal system was a taller order.

RBG wasn't sure she could find Sweden on a map. But she knew how she felt about writing a book of her own. And though she only half-realized it at the time, there was another reason she took Smit up on his offer. Jane was in first grade. RBG was nearing thirty, and she had never lived alone, or spent much time on her own at all. She wondered if she could cut it. Marty agreed to hold down the home front, and he and Jane would eventually come visit.

At the airport in Stockholm, Swedish city judge Anders Bruzelius, who had arrived to fetch her, walked right by her, expecting a much older woman. Nevertheless, RBG had arrived at the right time. In the postwar era, Swedish women had begun to enter the workforce in large numbers, more than American women had. They found their liberation to be partial. Journalist Eva Moberg spoke for many Swedish women when, in a 1961 essay, she demanded to know why women now had two jobs while men had one. "Actually, there is no biological connection whatsoever between the function of giving birth to and nursing a child and the function of washing its clothes, preparing its food, and trying to bring it up to be a good and harmonious person," Moberg wrote. "Both men and women have one main role:

that of being human beings." In the summer of 1962, during one of RBG's trips, another American woman arrived in Sweden. Actress Sherri Finkbine had tried to get an abortion after taking the then-common sleep aid thalidomide, which doctors belatedly realized caused severe fetal disabilities. Abortion was still broadly illegal in the United States, and only Sweden opened its doors to Finkbine.

When RBG wasn't immersing herself in the Swedish legal system or watching Ingmar Bergman movies sans subtitles, she observed these debates in awe. Who knew another world was possible for women—one in which they could work, fight back at unfair conditions, end a pregnancy if they felt they needed to? One where the government, pushed by activists, had begun to take an active interest in freeing men and women from prescribed gender roles? It was a personal revolution for her too. She found out in her first six weeks on her own that she could do just fine.

Back in New York, Smit encouraged her to teach some civil procedure classes at Columbia and to overcome her shyness by speaking at international conferences. She and Bruzelius published their book on Swedish civil procedure, later called the best English-language book on the Swedish judicial system. (True, at the time, it was the only one.) She felt surer of herself, but there was too much going on to think about it much. It would be a few years before RBG realized just how much she had learned in Sweden. It would change her life.

4

STEREOTYPES OF A LADY MISUNDERSTOOD

"So it was that ten years of my life that I devoted to litigating cases about—I don't say women's rights—I say the constitutional principle of the equal citizenship stature of men and women."

—RBG, 2010

RBG HAD SKIPPED LUNCH the morning of January 17, 1973. She was afraid she would vomit. Wearing her mother's pin and earrings, like a soldier suiting up for battle, RBG stood alone in front of nine stone-faced men and asked them to do something they had until then refused to do. Recognize that the Constitution banned sex discrimination.

All oral arguments at the Supreme Court begin the same way: "Mr. Chief Justice, and may it please the court." You can listen to the recording of RBG speaking these words, how at first they came out a little shakily. It was her first time arguing before the court.

To still the queasiness in her stomach, she had memorized the opening sentence. She told the justices about Sharron Frontiero, an air force lieutenant whose husband, Joseph, had been denied the same housing, medical, and dental benefits as other military spouses, simply because Sharron was a woman and Joseph was a man.

Fourteen months earlier, the court had ruled on the case of an Idaho woman denied the right to administer her dead son's estate because she was a woman. The justices said in *Reed v. Reed* that the state couldn't automatically assume men were better equipped to handle an estate than women. But they had left unsettled the broader question of whether discriminating on the basis of sex was almost always unconstitutional. RBG took a deep breath and told the justices they had to finish the job they started.

At Rutgers School of Law,
where RBG began teaching in 1963

The state law in *Reed* and the federal one she challenged that day in *Frontiero v. Richardson*, RBG argued, drew on "the same stereotype. The man is or should be the independent partner in a marital unit. The woman, with an occasional exception, is dependent, sheltered from bread-winning experience."

RBG usually looked for Marty in a room anytime she had to speak in public, but this time she had to settle for knowing he was behind her, in the section reserved for lawyers admitted to argue before the Supreme Court.

Suddenly, she felt the ground steady under her. These men, the most important judges in the country, were her captive audience for the next ten minutes. RBG knew so much more about the case and the topic than they did. She had to teach them. She knew how to do that. RBG had been teaching law for almost a decade.

"Mrs. Ruth Ginsburg" read the Supreme Court bar admissions card she had been handed in the court that day. RBG had gone by Ms. since there had been a Ms. The students in her Columbia seminar who had come along that day grimaced and wanted her to demand a change. She would not. RBG was there to win, not to rock the boat when it wasn't strictly necessary.

Her argument was radical enough. These distinguished men of the court thought of themselves as good fathers and good husbands. Men and women were fundamentally different, they believed, and women were lucky to be spared the squalor and pressures of the real world. This little woman, not yet forty, had to make the justices see that women deserved the same standing in the world as men.

Treating men and women differently under the law, RBG told the justices, implied a "judgment of inferiority." It told women their work and their families were less valuable. "These distinctions have a common effect," RBG said sternly. "They help keep woman in her place, a place inferior to that occupied by men in our society."

Behind her sat Brenda Feigen, who had cofounded the ACLU's Women's Rights Project with RBG one year earlier. Feigen had casebooks open on the desk before her, ready to provide RBG with a citation if she needed it. But RBG didn't need it. She rattled off the page numbers and volumes as casually as if she were giving a friend her phone number.

Her opponent that day was the federal government. In a brief, the government defended its policy of assuming women were dependents and allowing only a narrow pool of men to apply for dependent benefits. After all, most breadwinners were men. On the first page of that brief was the name of Erwin Griswold, RBG's old Harvard Law dean, now the nation's solicitor general. She'd come a long way from telling Dean Griswold she'd gone to law school to better make wifely chitchat with Marty.

The justices still hadn't said a word. RBG continued: "Sex, like race, is a visible, immutable characteristic bearing no necessary relationship to ability." The analogy had special meaning in the constitutional context: In a series of cases triggered by *Brown v. Board of Education*, the court had said that laws that classified on the basis of race were almost always unconstitutional, or deserving "strict scrutiny." The court had said in *Reed* that it wasn't applying strict scrutiny, but then it seemed to do so anyway. Were laws that classified what men and women could do blatantly unconstitutional the way laws classifying by race were? RBG boldly urged the court to say they were.

Her time was almost up. RBG looked the justices in the eye and quoted Sarah Grimké, the abolitionist and advocate for women's suffrage. "She spoke not elegantly, but with unmistakable clarity," RBG said. "She said, 'I ask no favor for my sex. All I ask of our brethren is that they take their feet off our necks.'"

Lawyers arguing at the Supreme Court sometimes have trouble getting out a full sentence. That January day, on an empty stomach and with Brooklyn vowels still in her voice, RBG spoke for ten minutes without a single interruption from the justices. She had stunned them into silence.

Underneath her composure, RBG was trembling. Were the justices even listening? She would have to wait five months to find out. As the crowd filed out after the argument, a stocky figure approached RBG. It was Dean Griswold, who had been watching one of his men argue against RBG and the other lawyer representing Frontiero. Solemnly, Griswold shook RBG's hand. That night, Justice Harry Blackmun, who in his diary graded lawyers on their performance before the court, gave RBG only a C+. "Very precise female," Blackmun wrote.

LAND, LIKE WOMAN, WAS MEANT TO BE POSSESSED

Ten years earlier, in 1963, RBG picked fewer battles. She had read and been awed by Simone de Beauvoir's *The Second Sex*. Like most of the things she learned in Sweden that were not civil procedure, she shelved it. A professor at Columbia, where she had begun lecturing, said he'd heard Rutgers School of Law was looking for a woman. After all, their only black professor had just moved on. No one seemed concerned that Columbia's law school had no female or black full-time faculty. Only fourteen women in the entire country had tenure-track positions at law schools, and Rutgers already had one of them. RBG and fellow Rutgers law professor Eva Hanks would soon be profiled in the *Newark Star-Ledger* under the headline "Robes for Two Ladies." The story led with calling them "slim, attractive" and gushed, "from their youthful appearance, they could easily be taken for students."

In her first year, Rutgers offered RBG an annual contract to teach civil procedure. The salary was low. After all, Dean Willard Heckel reminded her, it was a state school, and she was a woman. "They told me, 'We can't pay you as much as A., who has five children; you have a husband who earns a good salary,'" RBG remembered, discreetly withholding names. "I asked if B., a bachelor, was also paid more, and was told, 'yes.'" That was the end of that conversation. RBG kept her head down, taking the train each day to Newark from Manhattan's Penn Station and publishing articles with titles like "Recognition and Execution of Foreign Civil Judgments and Arbitration Awards." She made it to a second year.

Then came a surprise. After Marty's surgery, but before his radiation for testicular cancer, the doctor had informed the couple they had a quick and final window to try for a second child. Those were the days of juggling law school and a toddler and not knowing how long Marty would live. Another child was something they couldn't imagine. By the time Jane was nearly ten years old, her parents had just about convinced her that being an only child wasn't such a bad thing. But early in 1965, RBG discovered she was pregnant. "Tell me, dear," said the female doctor, taking RBG's hand. "Is there another?" There was no other. They ran a test and confirmed that Marty was still able to produce sperm.

RBG's joy at the news of her pregnancy was tangled up in anxiety about her job. Rutgers would decide on her contract renewal at the end of the spring semester, and RBG wasn't about to repeat the mistake she had made at the Social Security office in Oklahoma. She ran to her mother-in-law's closet. Evelyn Ginsburg wore one size larger, and with a due date in September, RBG might only begin showing during the summer vacation. It worked. RBG waited until the last day of classes, with the next year's contract in her hand, to break the news to her fellow professors. James was born September 8. Professor Ginsburg was soon back before her students as if nothing had changed.

But some things had changed. One of her law students declared himself a member of the free speech movement. "Each day, just before class, he climbed up on a branch, perched himself there, then thumbed his nose at me intermittently," RBG recalled. In her first classes at Rutgers, there had been maybe five or six women on every seating chart. As more men suited up for Vietnam, more women filled law school seats. Outside the classroom, *The Feminine Mystique,* chronicling the discontent of educated middle-class women with their domestic roles, had sold over a million copies in its first paperback printing. The Civil Rights Act of 1964 had almost by accident banned employment discrimination on the basis of sex alongside race, despite many ball-and-chain jokes from congressmen. (Representative Emanuel Celler joked that he usually had the last word in his house: "Yes, dear.")

The New Jersey branch of the American Civil Liberties Union, where RBG had signed up as a volunteer lawyer, was overwhelmed by letters from women. She was a woman, RBG was told, couldn't she handle it? She dutifully took a look. A woman who worked at Lipton Tea was barred from adding her family to her health insurance plan because the company as-

RBG at Rutgers

sumed only married men had dependents. Girls weren't welcome in Princeton's summer engineering program. The best tennis player in Teaneck, New Jersey, wasn't allowed on the varsity team because she was a girl. Some letters gave RBG the embarrassed flush of recognition. Teachers complained that they were forced off the job the moment they started showing pregnancy, and sometimes before. The schools called it maternity leave, but it wasn't voluntary or paid, and the teachers couldn't get their jobs back unless the school felt like it. One military woman had received an honorable discharge for being pregnant, but when she tried to reenlist, she learned pregnancy was a "moral and administrative disqualification." None of these problems were new. What was new was that anyone thought it was worth it to complain about it. RBG certainly hadn't.

The new crop of female law students, a decade or so younger than her, did more than complain. They made demands. Some of them were fresh from Mississippi, working for civil rights with the Student Nonviolent Coordinating Committee. These women had seen lawyers help lead the way, only to come to law schools and find that ladies were expected to fall in line. The universities themselves began to grudgingly make more space for women, especially after 1968, when the Johnson administration added sex discrimination to the list of sins that would imperil federal funding.

RBG watched these female students with some awe. How different they were from her generation, who'd been terrified of making a splash. When a handful of students came to RBG in 1970 and asked her to teach the first-ever Rutgers class on women and the law, she was ready to agree. It took her only about a month to read every federal decision and every law review article about women's status. There wasn't much. One popular textbook included the passage "Land, like woman, was meant to be possessed." (The book was about land ownership; women were just the analogy.) When she left the library, RBG knew this much: Her days of quiet acceptance were over. That included accepting Rutgers's giving her the ladies' discount. RBG helped the other female professors file a federal class-action pay-discrimination claim against the university. They won.

PLUCKING HERSELF
OUT OF OBSCURITY

On August 20, 1971, a female letter carrier in Springfield, New Jersey, wrote to the New Jersey chapter of the ACLU to complain that she wasn't allowed to wear the same hat that men wore. "The female carrier hats, a beret or a pillbox, have no place on which to attach my badge," Laney Kaplan explained in her letter. "The male carrier hat has a brim to keep the sun from your eyes, which the female carrier hats have none."

RBG was getting ready to lecture at Harvard Law School for the semester. She had begun bringing cases to the Supreme Court. But no case was too small. "The insistence on sexual identification by headgear for female letter carriers at the expense of functional features that would facilitate job performance appears to be wholly arbitrary," RBG wrote the postmaster general. The man may not have known what hit him.

It was clear to RBG that fighting discrimination one strongly worded letter at a time was like catching the ocean in a thimble.

RBG at the ACLU of New Jersey

There would always be another sexist law or regulation to take down. Women's rights advocates needed to think bigger. What the country needed was a broader recognition of gender equality, whether in headgear or federal policy. For decades, some feminists had said the solution was an equal rights amendment to the Constitution, which would read, *"Equality of rights under the law shall not be denied or abridged by the United States or by any state on account of sex."*

This amendment, known as the ERA, had been introduced in every session of Congress since 1923, but each time it had been held up in committee. RBG wondered whether the Constitution already held the answer. Its preamble began with "We the people," and women were people, even if they had been long prevented from living out their full destinies. Didn't women deserve equal protection under the law, as the Fourteenth Amendment promised? The question was how to get at least five Supreme Court justices to see the Constitution as she did. By the early seventies, women's roles had fundamentally transformed almost everywhere but in the high court's chambers. Maybe, given the right case, the justices would come around.

RBG was puzzling over her strategy one night, working, as she usually did, in the bedroom. "There's something you've got to read," Marty exclaimed from the dining room, where he was working. "I don't read tax cases," RBG replied. She would be glad she read that one.

Charles E. Moritz was a traveling salesman who lived with his eighty-nine-year-old mother in Denver. Moritz paid someone to care for her when he was on the road, but his troubles began when he tried to take a tax deduction. The IRS only granted such deductions to women, widowers, or the husbands of incapacitated women, and Moritz was a never-married man. The idea that a man on his own might be responsible somehow for caregiving apparently never crossed the government's mind. With a wide grin, RBG said, "Let's take it." It was her and Marty's first professional partnership.

On the surface, the Moritz case was more small ball. He had been denied no more than six hundred dollars in expenses. There was no apparent glaring injustice to women. Marty and RBG could see beyond that. The government was senselessly denying a benefit to someone purely on the basis of gender. If the court said that was wrong, the precedent set would open the door to a broader recognition of gender equality.

RBG wrote to Mel Wulf, an old friend from summer camp who had become the national legal director for the ACLU, seeking support. Wulf agreed to back them. He later told author Fred Strebeigh that he knew that RBG was doing "some down and dirty women's rights work" out in New

RBG at work

Jersey. Wulf was about to "pluck her from obscurity," he bragged to Strebeigh. He would help her get to the Supreme Court.

In their brief, the Ginsburgs argued that the government couldn't discriminate between men and women "when biological differences are not related to the activities in question." RBG sent their work to Wulf. She knew the ACLU had taken on the Supreme Court appeal of an Idaho law that preferred men over women to be administrators of estates. Sally Reed's husband had been abusive and left the family, but when their son killed himself, it was Cecil Reed who would officially carry on what little material possessions the son had left behind, just because Cecil was a man. That was what the law said. RBG believed the Moritz case, paired with *Reed,* could show that gender discrimination harmed everybody.

"Some of this should be useful for *Reed v. Reed,*" she wrote Wulf on April 6, 1971, attaching the *Moritz* brief. "Have you thought about whether it would be appropriate to have a woman co-counsel in that case???" RBG had rarely asked anyone to consider her because she was a woman, but getting to the Supreme Court was worth it. Thinking it over years later, Wulf told Strebeigh, "Damn, maybe I didn't pluck her from obscurity. Maybe she plucked herself from obscurity." He was right. Wulf told RBG he could use her help building Sally Reed's case to the Supreme Court.

THE SUPREME COURT NEVER SAW A SEX CLASSIFICATION IT DIDN'T LIKE

The Reed case had high stakes. If the Supreme Court wasn't ready to overturn its precedents that allowed the law to treat women as second-class citizens, *Reed* might lead it to double down on bad law. Only ten years prior, in

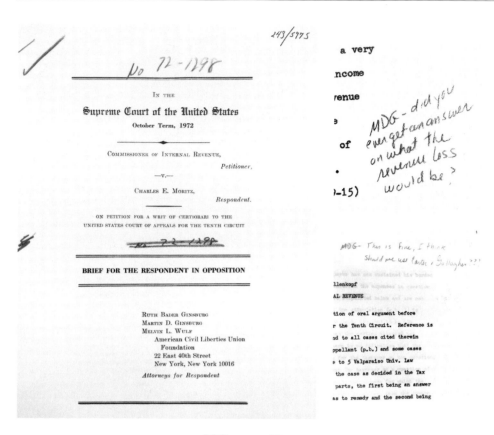

RBG's notes to Marty

1961, a woman named Gwendolyn Hoyt, tried for murdering her husband, had challenged the all-male jury that convicted her. In Florida, men were obliged to serve on juries, but women had to opt in. It was perfectly fine to treat women's participation as an afterthought, the justices said, because women were "still regarded as the center of home and family life." The Hoyt case made plain that the court hadn't progressed much since the 1948 opinion in which Felix Frankfurter—the same justice who refused to hire RBG as a clerk—gravely acknowledged that letting women freely bartend could "give rise to moral and social problems."

Back in law school, in her summer working at Paul Weiss, RBG had met a lawyer named Pauli Murray. She was a black woman at a time when race and gender were largely seen as separate categories. Murray worked passionately to build bridges between the civil rights movement, which she critiqued for being male-dominated, and women's rights activists, many of whom had serious blind spots on race. It turned out that even though RBG was asking the court to venture somewhere it had never gone, Murray had taken the first steps.

Murray had been arguing as early as 1961 that the equal protection clause of the Fourteenth Amendment might on its own free women of legal constraints. With fellow ACLU attorney Dorothy Kenyon, Murray tried to find a way to overturn the Hoyt precedent. "Jane Crow and the Law," a 1965 article Murray coauthored comparing racial and gendered oppression, was on RBG's Rutgers syllabus. The year after that article was published, Murray and Kenyon had tried to put their theories of the parallels and intersections of race and gender into practice. They challenged the all-white and all-male jury in Alabama that acquitted the murderers of two voting rights activists. They won, but Alabama never appealed to the Supreme Court, so the story ended there.

Murray's work was all over RBG's soon-to-be-famous *Reed* brief, which also included unusual references to Simone de Beauvoir, the poet Alfred Lord Tennyson, and

Civil rights activist Pauli Murray, who inspired RBG

13 to mail out
bring home 5 for me

RUTGERS · THE STATE UNIVERSITY

SCHOOL OF LAW

180 PLANE STREET
NEWARK, NEW JERSEY 07102

3)

Mailing list for Moritz

Melvin Wulf, Esq.   send 3 copies   to Wulf
American Civil Liberties Union
156 Fifth Ave
NY NY

Include note to Wulf:
  Dear Mel

  Some of this should be useful for Reed v. Reed.
Have you thought about whether it would be appropriate
to have a woman co-counsel in that case???

              Best regards
                 sign Ruth

                 RBG

the sociologist Gunnar Myrdal. Written with the help of RBG's feminist law students, the brief pointed out that while the world had changed, the law was stuck in the old ways. Before she submitted the *Reed* brief to the Supreme Court, RBG added two more names to the cover, where the authors' names went: Dorothy Kenyon and Pauli Murray. She wanted to make it clear that she was "standing on their shoulders," RBG later said.

"It's just not done," Burt Neuborne, then a colleague at the ACLU, remembers telling her. He called it a "violation of the canons."

"I don't care," RBG replied. "They deserve recognition." Later, she would say her work was carrying on what Kenyon and Murray had pioneered. It was just that the world was finally ready to listen.

70 - 4

Supreme Court, U.S.
FILED
JUN 25 1971
E. ROBERT SEAVER, CLERK

IN THE

Supreme Court of the United States

OCTOBER TERM 1970

SALLY M. REED,

Appellant,

—v.—

CECIL R. REED, Administrator, In the Matter of the Estate of Richard Lynn Reed, Deceased.

ON APPEAL FROM THE SUPREME COURT
OF THE STATE OF IDAHO

BRIEF FOR APPELLANT

MELVIN L. WULF
American Civil Liberties
Union Foundation
156 Fifth Avenue
New York, N. Y. 10010

RUTH BADER GINSBURG
Rutgers Law School
180 University Avenue
Newark, New Jersey

ALLEN R. DERR
817 West Franklin Street
Boise, Idaho 83701

PAULI MURRAY
504 Beacon Street
Boston, Mass. 02115

DOROTHY KENYON
433 W. 21st Street
New York, N. Y. 10011

Attorneys for Appellant

FROM RBG'S BRIEF
IN *REED V. REED* *

The sex line drawn by Sec. 15-314, mandating subordination of women to men without regard to individual capacity, creates a **"suspect classification"** requiring close judicial scrutiny. Although the legislature may distinguish between individuals on the basis of their need or ability, it is presumptively impermissible to distinguish on the basis of an unalterable identifying trait over which the individual has no control and for which he or she should not be disadvantaged by the law. Legislative discrimination grounded on sex, for purposes unrelated to any biological difference between the sexes, ranks with legislative discrimination based on race, another congenital, unalterable trait of birth, and merits no greater judicial deference.

The distance to equal opportunity for women in the United States remains considerable in face of the pervasive social, cultural and legal roots of sex-based discrimination. **As other groups that have been assisted toward full equality before the law via the "suspect classification" doctrine,** women are sparsely represented in legislative and policy-making chambers and lack political power to remedy the discriminatory treatment they are accorded in the law and in society generally. Absent firm constitutional foundation for equal treatment of men and women by the law, women seeking to be judged on their individual merits will continue to encounter law-sanctioned obstacles.

Prior decisions of this Court have contributed to the separate and unequal status of women in the United States. **But the national conscience has been awakened** to the

Groups that are deemed "suspect" are those that receive closer scrutiny by courts in equal protection challenges, making it much harder for the government to classify on the basis of such categories.

RBG is invoking the concept of historically disempowered groups deserving greater protection from the courts.

Women are marching in the streets, demanding equal rights, and can no longer be ignored.

* Thanks to Neil Siegel, professor of law and political science at Duke University, and Reva Siegel, professor of law at Yale Law School, for help with the commentary on this excerpt as well as for commentary on the *Struck v. Secretary of Defense, United States v. Virginia,* and *Gonzales v. Carhart* excerpts.

sometimes subtle assignment of inferior status to women by the dominant male culture. . . .

The time is ripe for this Court to repudiate the premise that, with minimal justification, the legislature may draw **"a sharp line between the sexes,"** just as this Court has repudiated once settled law that differential treatment of the races is constitutionally permissible. . . .

Biological differences between the sexes bear no relationship to the duties performed by an administrator. Idaho's interest in **administrative convenience,** served by excluding women who would compete with men for appointment as an administrator, falls far short of a compelling state interest when appraised in light of the interest of the class against which the statute discriminates—an interest in treatment by the law as full human personalities. If sex is a "suspect classification," a state interest in avoiding a hearing cannot justify rank discrimination against a person solely on the ground that she is a female.

. . . **Laws which disable women from full participation in the political, business and economic arenas** are often characterized as **"protective"** and **beneficial.** Those same **laws applied to racial or ethnic minorities would readily be recognized as invidious and impermissible.** The pedestal upon which women have been placed has all too often, upon closer inspection, been revealed as a cage.

RBG is quoting Justice Felix Frankfurter, who refused to hire her as a clerk because she was a woman. This is from his opinion upholding the law restricting women from tending bar.

RBG wants to establish how irrational it is to claim that men and women are biologically destined to have rigid roles. What does any of this have to do with your body parts?

Equality was just too inconvenient, according to Idaho. Not a good enough excuse, says RBG.

So-called protective legislation for the work conditions of women and children included safety standards, but also limited wages, working hours, and opportunities.

#benevolentsexism

RBG would later stop making this sort of argument as she, in her own words, became "more sensitive to the distinctions— that all oppressed people are not oppressed in the identical way or to the same degree."

On November 22, 1971, RBG lifted her head briefly from her reading. She was coming home by train, exhausted. Her eye fell on a man's newspaper. "High Court Outlaws Sex Discrimination" blared the front page of the *New York Post*. Not exactly, she learned when she finally got her hands on the opinion. The court had ruled for Sally Reed, the first time the Supreme Court ever struck down a law that treated men and women unequally. It was a big deal. But the decision's reach was ambiguous. The court had laid down no broader rule. RBG's work was only just beginning.

THE BIRTH OF THE WRP

Early mailings from the ACLU Women's Rights Project bore an unlikely stamp: the Playboy Bunny. At least one recipient was outraged at what turned out to be an in-kind donation from the magazine's foundation, a big ACLU donor. The feminist spin-off had begun on a shoestring. The WRP's first full-time employee was Brenda Feigen, a Harvard Law School graduate who had become a feminist activist. RBG's law students pitched in on the legwork.

Still, RBG had big plans for the project, which she'd proposed to the ACLU board right after she won *Reed*. Along with Hugh Hefner, Erwin Griswold was a surprise, if unofficial, benefactor. After the Ginsburgs won the Moritz case at the Tenth Circuit Court of Appeals, Solicitor General Griswold protested to the Supreme Court that the justices had to overrule them; other-

RBG split her time between Columbia and the ACLU.

wise, hundreds of federal laws might be deemed unconstitutional. To prove his point, Griswold attached a computer-generated list, marked Appendix E, of all the laws and regulations that treated men and women differently. RBG swiftly realized what Appendix E really was: a hit list.

The country had new laws banning discrimination in pay, employment, and education. But RBG knew that promises on paper wouldn't be enough. "The distance to equal opportunity for women—in the face of the pervasive social, cultural, and legal roots of sex-based discrimination—remains considerable," she wrote in a prospectus in October 1972. The WRP would have three missions: public education, changing the law, and bringing cases to court, with the help of local ACLU affiliates across the country.

Getting to equality would mean attacking on every front. Even if the Supreme Court made abortion legal, as it had just been asked to do, "excessive restrictions on where abortions can be performed and medical benefits that can be applied to abortions would still have to be challenged." Other priorities, RBG wrote, would be "the right to be voluntarily sterilized"—something white, middle-class women had been discouraged from doing by their doctors—"and the right not to be involuntarily sterilized"—something women of color and those considered "mentally defective" had been subject to. The project, wrote RBG, would tackle discrimination in education and training programs, as well as in the availability of mortgages, credit cards, loans, and home rentals; serve women in prison and in the military; and take on "discriminatory confinement of girls in juvenile institutions because of sexual promiscuity." It would also go after institutions that discriminated against pregnant women.

On May 14, 1973, the Supreme Court ruled on *Frontiero v. Richardson,* the first case RBG had argued before the court herself. Technically, she won again: The justices struck down the rule that treated Sharron Frontiero's work as less important to her family than a male servicemember's. And Justice William Brennan's opinion *sounded* like a win. "Traditionally, such discrimination was rationalized by an attitude of 'romantic paternalism' which, in practical effect, put women not on a pedestal, but in a cage," he wrote, taking the words right from feminist lawyers' mouths. But there weren't five votes for a broader rule that would make most classifications by gender unconstitutional. Justice William Rehnquist was the lone dissenter. He told the *Los Angeles Times,* "My wife became resigned long ago to the idea that she married a male chauvinist pig, and my daughters never pay attention to anything I do."

RBG learned a lesson that would stay with her for the rest of her life. She had been trying to teach the justices, and she wouldn't give up. But as she later acknowledged, "one doesn't learn that lesson in a day. Generally, change in our society is incremental, I think. Real change, enduring change, happens one step at a time." She would have to be patient. She would have to be strategic. And maybe a little deaf.

At the ACLU's Women's Rights Project

Her fellow feminists, on fire to transform the world, sometimes had to be persuaded to see things her way. "She insisted that we attempt to develop the law one step at a time," fellow ACLU lawyer Kathleen Peratis later said. "'Present the court with the next logical step,' she urged us, and then the next and then the next. 'Don't ask them to go too far too fast, or you'll lose what you might have won.' She often said, 'It's not time for that case.' We usually followed her advice, and when we didn't, we invariably lost."

PROFESSOR GINSBURG

RBG had begun to make a name for herself, even though she rarely sought the limelight. "Ginsburg lacks the dash of a Gloria Steinem, or the physical power of a Betty Friedan," wrote one student profiler. "Her hair is usually tied in a ponytail. She speaks flatly, sometimes haltingly, but always precisely. She dresses conservatively. Among themselves, students call her Ruthie, as if she were someone's Jewish aunt. They are able to feel close to her without knowing her that well." RBG's students wrote in one course evaluation that she was "brilliant" and an "excellent teacher" but also "distant towards students" and "quite a reserved person."

By 1972, Columbia, which had let RBG go west to Rutgers nine years earlier, finally saw her value. Her alma mater offered her the chance to become the law school's first tenured female professor, which she accepted with the understanding that she would spend part of her time at the ACLU. The *New York Times* said Columbia had "scored a major coup: its law school, to its undisguised glee, has just bid for and won a woman for the job of full professor." After all, according to the dean of the law school, "Mrs. Ginsburg" was actually qualified, apparently unlike all the other women they had refused to hire in 114 years of existence. ("Just one point about which I am curious," RBG wrote the reporter when the piece came out. "Did the *Times* rule out Ms.?")

RBG struck a surprisingly blunt note in the story. "The only confining thing for me is time. I'm not going to curtail my activities in any way to please them," she said, apparently referring to the faculty and administration. "I don't think I'll have any problem," she added a moment later. "People will be pleasant on the outside. Some of them may have reservations about what I'm doing, but I don't think they'll be expressed."

Some people did have reservations, but the women at Columbia had been waiting for her. Almost immediately, they began contacting her to air grievances. Did RBG know that Columbia employees didn't have pregnancy

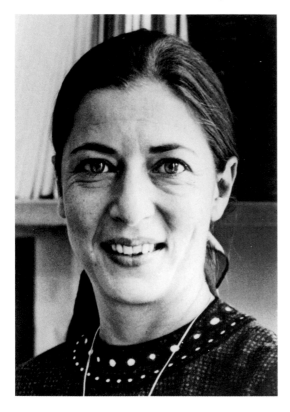

At Columbia in 1972

coverage and that women got lower pension benefits and lower pay? Well, now that she did, RBG helped file a class-action lawsuit with one hundred named plaintiffs on behalf of female teachers and administrators at the university. They won. Did RBG know that the university was about to lay off more than two dozen maids, all women, but not a single janitor? "We feel that our hope in preventing these firings lies in getting visible the support that we know exists for these women on this campus," wrote the activists on behalf of the maids, most of whom were women of color.

RBG wrote to Columbia's president, calling the firing of the maids a "grave and costly mistake" and urged him to "avoid a course destined to turn into a federal case." She went to meetings to press the maids' case. She even got the ACLU and its New York branch involved, much to the indignation of Walter Gellhorn, the Columbia Law professor who had helped RBG get her job at Rutgers. In a letter addressed to the "gentlemen" of the ACLU, Gellhorn accused the group of too quickly accusing the university of sex discrimination. (RBG scrawled furiously in the letter's margins, "He misconceives nature of the case. No!!!")

"The present episode," Gellhorn said, made him fear that the group had "tended too much to begin screaming prematurely." The word *mansplaining* was, unfortunately, decades away from being invented. But in the end, no one, maid or janitor, was fired.

RBG had tenure, but she didn't have to pick these battles, especially when some of her colleagues regarded her with suspicion for being there at all. "There was a certain hostility to having her there, and the notion that she was only there because of the pressure the school faced to hire a woman,"

RBG was the first tenured woman at Columbia Law School.

recalls Diane Zimmerman, a student at Columbia Law at the time whom RBG mentored. RBG knew people said "affirmative action" like it was an insult. "Others were of the view," she later wrote, "that at last, the days of 'negative action' were over."

THE WOMAN WHO DIDN'T WANT AN ABORTION

"Women Working." Brenda Feigen hung a bright yellow sign on the door with those words to mark WRP's territory at the new ACLU offices on Fortieth Street. RBG loved that sign. Women working at the WRP also meant the literal arrival of newborn babies, breast-fed during the day by their attorney moms, tended by paid college students the rest of the time. Amid the chaos, RBG sat working methodically, her desk an oasis of calm. It was all a long way from getting pushed out of her job in Oklahoma, or scrambling for baggy clothes to keep her job at Rutgers.

That was inside the ACLU. Outside it, making reproductive freedom a reality was a knotty mess. The problem the WRP faced in connecting pregnancy to their line of sex-discrimination cases was this: Even if a man could take care of the kids and the elders, and a woman could join the air force and handle the family finances, only one of them could get pregnant and give birth. RBG and her team had to convince the justices that pregnancy too was a matter of equality—or inequality—and not just something special that women indulged in, off on their own. Even more radically, RBG wanted the Supreme Court to recognize that women would never be equal if they could not control their reproductive lives, whether they wanted to be pregnant or not. That meant the right to an abortion, and it meant the right to be free of discrimination for staying pregnant.

Captain Susan Struck, an air force nurse, never considered herself a feminist, but she also didn't behave like women were supposed to. For one thing, she had volunteered to be sent to Vietnam. In 1970, when she got pregnant, she refused to quit or get an abortion, the only options the military offered her. Ironically, abortion was still illegal almost everywhere in the United States, and it was a shock when, in 1969, radical feminists had held the first-ever abortion speak-out in a church basement in New York. Military bases were the exception. Struck, raised Catholic, had enough sick leave saved up to give birth and give her baby up for adoption. So Struck kept ignoring, then challenging, her discharge notices. She turned to the ACLU for help.

RBG jumped at the chance to build a gradual case that reproductive freedom was a condition of equality, beginning with a woman who didn't want an abortion. She couldn't help but notice the hypocrisy of a country that banned abortion except when it was convenient for the military. Other ACLU lawyers were involved in two more direct attacks on statewide abortion bans, *Doe v. Bolton* and *Roe v. Wade,* that were pending that very same Supreme Court term. Mindful of the arguments that had worked seven years earlier when the court struck down a contraception ban in *Griswold v. Connecticut,* the *Roe* and *Doe* briefs claimed abortion fell under a right to privacy, not equality. RBG had other ideas, as she made clear in the brief to the highest court for one of her favorite cases.

FROM RBG'S BRIEF IN *STRUCK V. SECRETARY OF DEFENSE*

"**The Air Force regulation** . . . directing immediate discharge of a woman officer upon determination that she is pregnant, reflects arbitrary notions of a woman's place wholly at odds with contemporary legislative and judicial recognition **that individual potential must not be restrained, nor equal opportunity limited, by law-sanctioned stereotypical prejudgments;** operating on the basis of characteristics assumed to typify pregnant women, and . . . in total disregard of individual capacities and qualifications, the regulation violates the due process clause of the fifth amendment to the United States Constitution.

The regulation singles out pregnancy, a physical condition unique to women involving a normally brief period of disability, as cause for immediate involuntary discharge. **No other physical condition occasioning a period of temporary disability, whether affecting a man or a woman, is similarly treated.** . . .

Heading the list of arbitrary barriers that have plagued women seeking equal opportunity is disadvantaged treatment based on their unique childbearing function. **Until very recent years, jurists have regarded any discrimination in the treatment of pregnant women and mothers as "benignly in their favor."** But in fact, restrictive rules, and particularly discharge for pregnancy rules, operate as "built-in headwinds" that drastically curtail women's opportunities. **Decisions of this Court that span a century have contributed to this anomaly: presumably well-meaning exaltation of woman's unique role in bearing children has, in effect, restrained women from developing their**

The policy: "A woman officer will be discharged from the service with the least practicable delay when a determination is made by a medical officer that she is pregnant." In other words, abort your pregnancy or lose your job.

RBG in a nutshell. Here she is connecting her ideas about pregnancy with her ideas about sex discrimination.

The idea was that if pregnancy was treated like other temporary disabilities rather than something singular, women wouldn't be singled out for discrimination. After all, men got injured or sick and had to take time off too. Why was women's time off any different?

"Benign" pregnancy policies included being forced off the job the moment pregnant women started showing. Two years after this was written, the Supreme Court would strike down a policy like that in Cleveland Board of Education v. LaFleur.

From the beginning, RBG viewed women's role in reproduction as a key source of societal discrimination that equal protection should forbid.

individual talents and capacities and has impelled them to accept a dependent, subordinate status in society.

In addition to its reliance on a sex-based stereotype no less invidious than **one racial or religious,** the regulation invoked against petitioner operates as an unconstitutional infringement upon petitioner's right to privacy in the conduct of her personal life and her right to free exercise of her religion. It "encourages" women officers not to bear children by prohibiting them from remaining in the Air Force if they do. **Men in the Air Force, on the other hand, are not "encouraged," on pain of discharge, to avoid the pleasures and responsibilities entailed in fathering children. A man serves in the Air Force with no unwarranted governmental intrusion into the matter of his sexual privacy or his decision whether to beget a child. The woman serves subject to "regulation"; her pursuit of an Air Force career requires that she decide not to bear a child. . . .**

Although petitioner, a Roman Catholic, does not seek privileged treatment based on her religious orientation, it should be stressed that the challenged regulation operates with particularly brutal force against women of her faith. . . . Termination of pregnancy prior to the birth of a living child was not an option petitioner could choose. **Thus, the regulation pitted her Air Force career against her right to privacy and autonomy in sexual matters, as well as her religious conscience.**

. . . The conclusion is inescapable that the regulation directing Captain Struck's discharge reflects blatant prejudice against women for a condition peculiar to their sex. . . . If involuntary discharge of a woman solely on the ground of her pregnancy is not sex discrimination, nothing is!

On December 4, 1972, the same day she filed her brief to the Supreme Court in the Struck case, RBG got some bad news. Solicitor General Griswold had seen a loss coming and persuaded the air force to change its policy of automatically discharging pregnant women. The case was dismissed as moot. But RBG wasn't ready to let go. She asked Struck, by then marooned at Minot Air Force Base in North Dakota, if there was any way to keep the case alive.

Struck dreamed of being a pilot. They had a big laugh over that one, Struck and RBG. A female pilot? It was too impossible to even ask for.

DO THE DEED, PAY THE PRICE

Six weeks after the Struck case hit a wall, the Supreme Court handed down its twin decisions in *Roe* and *Doe*. Seven justices declared that the constitutional right to privacy "is broad enough to encompass a woman's decision whether or not to terminate her pregnancy," and struck down all fifty states' abortion laws. In the years that followed, RBG made no bones about her dislike of Justice Harry Blackmun's opinion in the case. "It's not about the woman alone," she remarked disdainfully. "It's the woman in consultation with her doctor. So the view you get is the tall doctor and the little woman who needs him." Worse, the very sweep of the opinion violated RBG's go-slow policy, which she believed was the only way to change minds.

The Supreme Court had chosen a path that led it away from where RBG had been hoping to coax the justices, and there seemed to be no turning back. If abortion was a private choice, would public insurance have to pay for it like any other medical procedure? No, said the Supreme Court seven years after *Roe*, when it upheld a ban on federal funding for abortion. The burden of "privacy" fell on poor women's shoulders. What if a woman wanted to stay pregnant, like Struck? Was her right to continue working free from discrimination protected by the right to privacy? That answer came even sooner.

Employers had long refused to hire or promote women because they might get pregnant, forced them to take unpaid leave if they did get pregnant, and then refused to give women their jobs back when they were ready to return to work. Such treatment, RBG argued, made assumptions about women's God-given roles just like the laws struck down in *Reed* and *Frontiero* did. They were "grounded on stereotypes concerning women's physical limitations and 'proper place' in society," RBG wrote in an amicus brief in one of a string of pregnancy-related cases before the Supreme Court in the seventies. "These employer policies," RBG wrote, had nothing to do with "the 'nature' of women or the realities of pregnancy."

That many of these women *needed* to work when pregnant and parenting didn't seem to register. "The notion is that when the woman gets pregnant, she's going to stay home and take care of her baby, everything's wonderful, and she's going to have a husband to support her," RBG said in 1977. "Well, the kinds of plaintiffs that came up in these cases were women who had no husbands. They were the sole support of themselves and the child to come." No matter their income, pregnant women were assumed to have taken themselves out of public life.

RBG also understood that how pregnant women were treated had to do with sex. Only a woman's body showed proof of having sex, and only women were punished for having it. She wrote to advise the lawyer of a pregnant servicewoman who had gotten a general discharge instead of an honorable one. "Surely the less than honorable

Ms.

September 13

Dear Ruth —
Thank you so much for the book, the idea of going to the conference, your excellent and effective argument — and most of all, just for being there.
You always make me very, very proud. And you change minds.
Best.
Gloria

A note from Ms. *magazine cofounder Gloria Steinem*

aspect is not 'getting pregnant' but the conduct," RBG wrote. "As for that, it takes two, and no man (or no woman, probably) is discharged for having sexual relations."

The Supreme Court stubbornly refused to listen to any of this. Excluding pregnancy from a disability plan wasn't necessarily discriminating against women, the justices claimed in 1974 with *Geduldig v. Aiello*, because not all women are pregnant, even though all pregnant people are women. In another case, female employees sued General Electric, a company that had once made all women quit upon marrying, for excluding pregnancy coverage on its employee plan. GE's lawyer told the Supreme Court with a straight face that, after all, women didn't have to be pregnant. If they wanted to work, GE's attorney suggested, women now had legal access to what he called "an in-and-out noon-hour treatment." He meant abortion.

Astonishingly, on December 7, 1976, a majority of the Supreme Court agreed. Rehnquist wrote for the majority that pregnancy was special, because unlike race or gender itself, it was often "voluntarily undertaken and desired." The message was clear: Once you did the deed, you had to pay the price—that is, if you were a woman. Justices William Brennan and Thurgood Marshall protested in their dissent that GE hadn't left out any "so-called 'voluntary' disabilities including sport injuries, attempted suicides, venereal disease, disabilities incurred in the commission of a crime or during a fight, and elective cosmetic surgery."

Within a day of the General Electric decision, RBG called a meeting to map out a Plan B to protect pregnant workers from discrimination. "She was very much a leader of the coalition," says fellow feminist lawyer Judith Lichtman. "It only took two years to overturn a really stinky—can I say 'shitty'?—decision," she added. In October 1978, Congress passed the Pregnancy Discrimination Act, which made clear that employers would be discriminating against women if they didn't treat pregnant workers like other temporarily disabled workers.

Some feminists wanted pregnancy to be recognized as essentially different from "sports injuries" or "elective cosmetic surgery." But RBG was adamant that treating pregnancy as special would backfire. She hoped gender-neutral policies would make it harder for employers to single women out for discrimination. Her experience and clients had convinced her that anything that looked like a favor to women would be used against them.

WHAT ABOUT THE MEN?

Monday, November 27, 1972

Social Security inequality

To the editor:

Your article about widowed men last week prompted me to point out a serious inequality in the Social Security regulations.

It has been my misfortune to discover that a male can not collect Social Security benefits as a woman can.

My wife and I assumed reverse roles. She taught for seven years, the last two at Edison High School. She paid maximum dollars into Social Security. Meanwhile, I, for the most part, played homemaker.

Last June she passed away while giving birth to our only child. My son can collect benefits but I, because I am not a WOMAN homemaker, can not receive benefits.

Had I been paying into Social Security and, had I died, she would have been able to receive benefits, but male homemakers can not. I wonder if Glora Steinem knows about this?

STEPHEN WIESENFELD,
Edison

Of all of her clients, RBG was fondest of Stephen Wiesenfeld, a single father whose wife had died in childbirth. Bringing his case to the Supreme Court was a chance to show that sexism hurt everybody. While Stephen "played homemaker," as the letter that brought him to RBG's attention put it, his wife, Paula, had worked as a teacher and paid into Social Security. But only widows could get "mother's benefits." The law, RBG wrote in her brief to the Supreme Court on Wiesenfeld's behalf, "reflects the familiar stereotype that, throughout this Nation's history, has operated to devalue women's efforts in the economic sector."

Her argument went even further. "Just as the female insured individual's status as breadwinner is denigrated," RBG wrote, "so the parental status of her surviving spouse is discounted. For the sole reason that appellee is a father, not a mother, he is denied benefits that would permit him to attend personally to the care of his infant son, a child who has no other parent to provide that care." Then she twisted the knife. Their young son, Jason Paul, RBG wrote, was another victim of a law that "includes children with dead fathers, but excludes children with dead mothers."

RBG found out she won her case by flipping through her car radio on her way to Columbia. "My first reaction was that I have to get hold of myself or I'll have an accident," she told a reporter that day. "Then when I got to Columbia, I went running through the halls kissing the students who had worked with me on the case. And I am normally a very unemotional person." She told another friend it had made her cry.

"Given the purpose of enabling the surviving parent to remain at home to care for a child, the gender-based distinction of [the law] is entirely irrational," Brennan wrote. Rehnquist, still a women's rights skeptic, concurred, saying he was voting to strike down the law because it harmed the baby. At least he had taken that half step. RBG wrote of the case, "*Wiesenfeld* is part of an evolution toward a policy of neutrality—a policy that will accommodate traditional patterns, but at the same time, one that requires removal of artificial constraints so that men and women willing to explore their full potential as humans may create new traditions by their actions."

She had perplexed and even angered some of her allies by bringing so many cases with male plaintiffs. After all, it was the Women's Rights Project, not the men's rights project. Much later, people would say RBG was a genius for presenting the male-dominated court with their brethren. The truth was more complicated. The choices men like Stephen Wiesenfeld made baffled, even angered the justices. Why would he want to act like a woman? In a way, it was easier to understand why a woman would want to act like a man. RBG firmly believed that for women to be equal, men had to be

On April 14, 1975 the decision in *Weinberger v. Wiesenfeld* will become final. We hope you will join us in a toast to that happy event on

Sunday, April 20
from 4:00 - 7:00

at 150 East 69 St. Apt. 2-G
N.Y., N.Y. 10021

R.S.V.P. to Ruth Bader Ginsburg
280-2036

free. Decades later, an unnamed guest at a dinner party told the *New York Times* that RBG had fiercely interrupted another guest who mentioned she'd worked on behalf of "women's liberation." "She turned on him and said, 'It is not women's liberation; it is women's and men's liberation.' I'd never seen her exercise such strength and vehemence."

Nor was she interested in letting only one or two women into the old boys' network. RBG firmly believed that more women in public life would benefit everyone, including men. "Men need to learn, and they do when women show up in their midst in numbers, not as one-at-a-time curiosities," RBG remarked at the twenty-fifth anniversary of women at Harvard Law School in 1978. "Men need the experience of working with women who demonstrate a wide range of personality characteristics, they need to become working friends with women."

By that point, the percentage of women in law schools had risen to 30 percent. Former Harvard dean Erwin Griswold was worried, he wrote RBG that year, even though, as he reminded her, he had "got women into the Harvard Law School as soon as I could after I became dean." Griswold fretted that "between the women, though, and the minorities, the number of places available for white men has sharply dropped. The time may come when some consideration will be given to their plight." RBG, whose daughter, Jane, was at that time enrolled at Harvard Law School, was unperturbed. She wrote that she was pretty sure more women

RBG in 1977

and people of color could enroll "without denying to white men of merit a fair chance to compete for places."

That day, triumphantly back at Harvard Law School, RBG looked out at young women, including her daughter, whose road had been smoother. RBG was glad of it. She would soon argue what would turn out to be her last case before the Supreme Court. Slowly but surely, she had built a set of precedents that had walked the justices in her direction, toward recognizing women as people.

In her speech, RBG allowed herself a little levity. "I understand some of the men come to HLS these days because"—here she paused—"what better place to find a suitable woman?

"All-male retreats are on the wane," RBG continued. "I expect, before very long, the old boys will find no escape at judges' conference tables."

She was right.

Case	What Was at Stake
The widower cases: *Kahn v. Shevin* (1974), *Weinberger v. Wiesenfeld* (1975), *Califano v. Goldfarb* (1977).	RBG represented men harmed by discriminatory federal and state laws. Mel Kahn said it was unfair that widows, but not widowers, could get a small exemption from property taxes. Stephen Wiesenfeld wanted to care full time for his son, but only widows could collect Social Security parental benefits. To get survivor's benefits under Social Security, Leon Goldfarb had to jump through hoops widows didn't have to.
The pregnancy cases: *Struck v. Secretary of Defense* (1972), *LaFleur v. Cleveland Board of Education* (1974), *Geduldig v. Aiello* (1974), *General Electric v. Gilbert* (1976).	Women were being forced to choose between their pregnancies and their jobs, whether in the military (*Struck*) or teaching (*LaFleur*). Pregnant women were also being excluded from disability insurance and pension plans.
Forced sterilization of black women: *Cox v. Stanton* (1973).	As a teen mom in North Carolina, Nial Ruth Cox had been forcibly sterilized through the state eugenics program, a widespread practice that particularly targeted black women. She walked into the ACLU WRP and asked for help.
The jury cases: *Edwards v. Healy* and *Taylor v. Louisiana* (1975), *Duren v. Missouri* (1979).	States had long made jury service for women optional, which criminal defendants challenged as violating their right to a fair trial and to equal protection under the law.
The near-beer case: *Craig v. Boren* (1976).	Oklahoma frat boys protested the constitutionality of the fact that in their state, women were allowed to buy low-alcohol beer at age eighteen when men had to wait until they were twenty-one.

"I think that men and women, shoulder to shoulder, will work together to make this a better world. Just as I don't think that men are the superior sex, neither do I think women are. I think that it is great that we are beginning to use the talents of all of the people, in all walks of life, and that we no longer have the closed doors that we once had."

—RBG

RIGHTS CASES

RBG's Role	Result
She took all three to the Supreme Court. The Kahn case landed in her lap by surprise; RBG later said she hated it. She preferred Wiesenfeld's case, because he wasn't trying to take any benefits from women. The widowers' experiences showed, RBG said at the *Goldfarb* oral argument, that "gender discrimination is a two-edged sword."	*Kahn* was RBG's first and last loss at the court: Widows were entitled to special breaks, said the justices, because of past discrimination. She had better luck with *Wiesenfeld* and *Goldfarb*.
Struck never made it to the Supreme Court, but RBG helped write amicus briefs for the pregnancy discrimination cases that did. She later explained, "Only women become pregnant; and if you subject a woman to disadvantageous treatment on the basis of her pregnant status . . . you would be denying her equal treatment under the law."	The Supreme Court agreed it was wrong to force schoolteachers off the job halfway into their pregnancies, but refused to bar discrimination against pregnant women in disability and pension benefits, because pregnancy was theoretically voluntary.
The ACLU WRP's brief, on which RBG is listed as a coauthor, argued that North Carolina had violated Cox's constitutional rights. The state eugenics board, they said, targeted Cox "because she is a woman, because she is black" and "as a method of punishing women who bear children out of wedlock." WRP cofounder Brenda Feigen traveled throughout the South with Gloria Steinem to interview Fannie Lou Hamer and other survivors of sterilization.	The case hit a dead end on a technicality. In 2002, the state finally apologized for one of the most sweeping forced-sterilization programs and, in 2014, began offering limited payments to victims.
She took the cases to the Supreme Court. RBG was passionate about jury cases, because making women's service optional implied that "women were the center of home and family life, so they could be spared from performing a prime obligation of citizenship." She held her tongue at the *Duren* oral argument when Rehnquist said, "You won't settle for putting Susan B. Anthony on the new dollar, right?"	She won the cases. "Such systematic exclusion of women that results in jury venires averaging less than 15% female violates the Constitution's fair cross-section requirement," the court ruled.
RBG thought the "thirsty boys" case was "something of an embarrassment," but gamely took it to the Supreme Court.	The beer guzzlers' case turned out to be a legal landmark. The court finally applied "intermediate scrutiny" to laws that discriminated on the basis of sex.

"I am fearful, or suspicious, of generalizations about the way women or men are. . . . They cannot guide me reliably in making decisions about particular individuals."

—RBG

5

DON'T LET 'EM HOLD YOU DOWN, REACH FOR THE STARS

"People often ask me, 'Well, did you always want to be a judge?'
My answer is it just wasn't in the realm of the possible until Jimmy
Carter became president and was determined to draw on the talent
of all of the people, not just some of them."

—RBG, 2010

LIKE A BRIDE. That's how RBG felt when Bill Clinton ushered her out to the Rose Garden to introduce her as his Supreme Court nominee. Instead of the traditional white, she wore an oversize navy blazer dress and a scrunchie that nearly dwarfed her head. What only a handful of people gathered there knew was that the match almost didn't happen. Less than twenty-four hours earlier, Clinton had been about to get on the phone and offer his first Supreme Court nomination to someone else. To yet another man.

No doubt could be read on Clinton's face that afternoon. He introduced RBG as a hero to the women's movement and a legal star. Above all, Clinton said, he'd chosen her for being a moderate, neither liberal nor conservative, someone whose "moral imagination has cooled the fires of her colleagues' discord.

"Ruth Bader Ginsburg cannot be called a liberal or a conservative; she has proved herself too thoughtful for such labels," the president said. "Having experienced discrimination," he added, "she devoted the next twenty years of her career to fighting it and making this country a better place for our wives, our mothers, our sisters, and our daughters." RBG would have added, "And our husbands, our fathers, our brothers, and our sons."

Marty got his own Clinton shout-out too, as the man whom RBG had married thirty-nine years before. ("As a very young woman," Clinton assured the crowd with a grin.) Clinton didn't mention the other role Marty had played: doing everything in his power to make sure that the president heard about a certain former women's rights lawyer serving as a Federal Court of Appeals judge right there in Washington. "I wasn't important at all," Marty later insisted, but his friend Carr Ferguson gave him away. "There were probably scores, maybe hundreds of us" who had been called to lobby on RBG's behalf—anyone they knew in Congress or the White House, in either party. And when Marty heard that RBG's longtime dislike of the *Roe* decision had earned her the vague reputation of not being trusted by feminists, he pressed into service all of her movement friends.

RBG had rarely aggressively sold herself for anything, even by proxy, but one of her clerks told her that if she just waited to be chosen, she might be twenty-fifth on the list. She had to admit to herself that she wanted this.

Fresh to the presidency, Clinton was having a rough time with any number of appointments, with a succession of political controversies and hasty withdrawals. By June 1993, it had been four months since Associate Justice Byron White announced his retirement from the Supreme Court. The names of several possible successors had leaked to the press, though not RBG's. She was in the running, but thought it might be over when White House Counsel Bernard Nussbaum told her she could feel free to go to a weekend wedding in Vermont. Then she got a call from Nussbaum, telling her to come back to meet with the president.

Another appeals court judge, Stephen Breyer, supposedly had a tax issue, something that had sunk other appointees, and Clinton didn't warm to him. (A year later, Clinton would apparently change his mind, nominating Breyer to the court.) Mario Cuomo, Clinton's favorite, backed out mere minutes before the president was about to offer it to him.

Meeting at the White House on Sunday, Clinton liked RBG immediately. Clinton's staff was relieved that Marty was a tax lawyer, assuming he would have all their affairs in order. In fact, it was RBG who handled all of their personal finances. When the Clinton vetters showed up at the Ginsburgs' apartment in the Watergate building to hurriedly riffle through their tax records, Marty did make them lunch.

According to communications staffer George Stephanopoulos, Clinton briefly worried that RBG's support for public funding of abortion would "push her out on the cultural left." But he had wanted a history-making candidate, and RBG had made history. Close to midnight, Clinton called RBG and told her he would nominate her to be an associate justice, the second woman ever to sit on the Supreme Court.

"Tomorrow morning, we'll have a little ceremony in the Rose Garden," Clinton told her. And of course, he added, "we would like you to make some remarks."

That shook RBG out of her euphoria. She went to her desk. Late night had always been her most productive time, anyway. There was something else she liked about the speediness of it all. "The White House handlers had no time to edit it or suggest changes," she said later of her first words to the nation, "and then I gave it just as I wrote it."

The day America met RBG, they saw a woman even many of her friends had never glimpsed. There was no sign of the solemn woman she was said to be behind the enormous, violet-tinted glasses that halved her face that afternoon, or in the ebullient grin. She thanked the women's movement "that opened doors for people like me," as well as "the civil rights movement of the 1960s from which the women's movement drew inspiration.

"The announcement the President just made is significant, I believe, because it contributes to the end of the days when women, at least half the talent pool in our society, appear in high places only as one-at-a-time performers," RBG said.

"I have a last thank-you," she said. "It is to my mother, Celia Amster Bader, the bravest and strongest person I have known, who was taken from me much too soon," she said. "I pray that I may be all that she would have been had she lived in an age when women could aspire and achieve and daughters are cherished as much as sons."

Even people who knew her well had never seen her be so emotional, so unguarded. By that point, Bill Clinton was wiping a tear from his cheek. RBG had gotten to carry on her mother's memory before the country. She had even helped a man defy gender stereotypes.

MILITANT FEMINIST INTERPRETATIONS

Sometime in the seventies, RBG had been interviewed for a federal district court judge position. The screening committee told her she wasn't qualified because she had no experience in financial securities. "I wonder how many gender-discrimination cases they have handled," RBG retorted, but only later, to her friend the legal reporter Nina Totenberg.

Anyway, RBG didn't want to be a district court judge, the evidence-heavy first stop for any federal suit. She was more interested in the broader legal questions raised by federal appeals courts. The Supreme Court only takes about seventy-five cases a year, out of ten thousand it is asked to hear, so appeals court judges just below it are often the final word on the law. Joining such a court had long involved knowing the right guy, or supporting the right guy's election. Even after clearing that hurdle, old-boy network bar associations guarded the doors. No wonder that when Jimmy Carter became president in 1977, just one woman served as an appeals court judge.

The Carter administration was determined to do better. Feminist lawyers scrambled to help, forming a new organization to vet judicial candidates on their own metric of commitment to equality. Suddenly, RBG knew a woman. The new group's president was Lynn Hecht Schafran, who had been RBG's Columbia Law School student and ACLU intern.

At Columbia in 1980

As she applied for judicial positions on both the Second Circuit, close to home, and the D.C. Circuit, RBG knew her feminist past might be held against her. In notes to herself labeled "Notes from 2d Circuit Interview," a whole page preemptively addressed any issues that might come up about "bias based on experiences." A list of qualities RBG drew up to describe herself sold the star litigator rather short. It focused not on her brilliant strategy or accomplishments but on her "high capacity for sustained work— accustomed to long hours, homework, extending day as long as necessary to accomplish task needed to be done." She bloodlessly referred to her "high quality standards for own work product" ("my own sternest critic") and put near the bottom that she was a "good (sympathetic) listener." Overall, RBG wrote, "I very much want to be considered on the basis of whatever merit I have, not on the basis of my sex, or views of people who are not in a very good position to evaluate my performance and potential." To paraphrase Sarah Grimké, she just wanted the committee to take their feet off her neck.

RBG did not make the cut for the Second Circuit, apparently because she had applied to two courts, despite being assured it wouldn't disqualify her. Her letters at the time show her disappointment. "I am heartened by the people and groups who have questioned the 'merit' system as it appears to be working (or not working) in some areas of the country," she wrote feminist lawyer Diane Blank in March 1979. Women in the law who were her protégées or admirers rallied to RBG's side. At least one was inside the Carter administration.

"I cannot exaggerate the feeling among women lawyers that all increases in numbers or victories are pyrrhic if Ruth is not appointed," wrote Assistant Attorney General Barbara Babcock to Attorney General Griffin Bell on March 12. "It will be viewed as a slap in the face that a woman who is so well qualified, and more than any woman applicant in the country, has 'paid her dues,' is not chosen." Babcock sent a blind carbon copy to RBG. Within a month, Ruth Bader Ginsburg's name was before the Senate Judiciary Committee.

RBG's fears that her women's rights work would be held against her were briefly borne out. Representative John Ashbrook, a conservative Ohio congressman, complained that she had "militant feminist interpretations." Ashbrook's words, RBG wrote her old law professor Herb Wechsler, were a "gross distortion of my views, testimony and articles, but I doubt he cares what I did say or write." Luckily, Ashbrook, as a member of the House, did not get a vote. In May 1979, Nina Totenberg rallied to her side in the pages of *Legal Times*. "Republican Judiciary Committee members have dragged their feet, and no firm hearing date has been set," Totenberg wrote. "The reason is that the nominee is not a he, but a she—and she is the architect of the legal strategy for the women's movement."

But in the end, only legendary segregationist senator Strom Thurmond voted against her in the Judiciary Committee. In the full Senate, RBG was confirmed unanimously on June 18, 1980. She didn't forget the students and feminist lawyers who had gotten her there. Her former Columbia Law mentee Diane Zimmerman remembers the exuberant party thrown by students and faculty. RBG sat on the floor giggling, eating Kentucky Fried Chicken out of a bucket.

Senate of the United States

IN EXECUTIVE SESSION

June 18, 1980

Resolved, That the Senate advise and consent to the following nomination:

Ruth Bader Ginsburg, of New York, to be United States Circuit Judge for the District of Columbia Circuit.

Attest:

THE WHITE HOUSE
JUN 18 1980
RECEIVED

THE WOMEN ARE AGAINST HER

Another, more staid celebration was held after RBG's swearing-in. She asked Gerald Gunther, her beloved Columbia Law professor who had had to blackmail a judge to hire her as a clerk, to speak. Gunther, the biographer of Judge Learned Hand, told the assembled that RBG would be a judge like Hand, "genuinely open-minded and detached," and "heedful of limitations stemming from the judge's own competence." *Sure,* said Republicans and Democrats alike, elbowing him knowingly. The card-carrying member of the ACLU was going to be a judicial moderate?

Gunther bet the skeptics five dollars that in a couple of years, RBG would "widely be seen as the most independent, thoughtful, modest judge on the bench," he later wrote. Within a couple of years, Gunther got a five-dollar bill in the mail, along with a clipping from the *Washington Post* describing RBG as a solid centrist.

RBG had gotten onto the D.C. Circuit just under the wire of the Carter presidency. A year into her term, it was clear she was a long way from the feminist law world. The Reagan and Bush years went on to stack the D.C. Circuit with staunch conservatives like Antonin Scalia, Kenneth Starr, Robert Bork, and Clarence Thomas. Her particular appeals court mostly oversaw federal agencies, and the work was often so intricately boring that Marty joked that most cases involved the Federal Energy Regulatory Commission. Sometimes called the second most important court in the country, the D.C. Circuit was also unmistakably a pipeline to the Supreme Court.

The new title did not erase some of the old indignities, however. At RBG's twenty-fifth Harvard Law School reunion, someone tried to organize the "members of the class and their wives" in a group photograph. "What do you mean, 'wives'?" demanded RBG. At cocktail parties, when the host would introduce someone to "Judge Ginsburg," a hand was usually outstretched to Marty.

As the eighties wore on, some of RBG's D.C. Circuit clerks had trouble even remembering that RBG had made her name litigating women's rights.

"She was widely regarded not as a 'women's' judge, much less a 'political' judge, but as a judge's judge," two of her former clerks, David and Susan Williams, later wrote, as if being a "women's judge" was something to shrink away from. RBG saw the role of an appeals court judge as fundamentally different than her old job; she was to follow precedent, not try to change it. And on a court where most decisions were made on a panel of three, RBG developed her fixation on compromise and collegiality.

"I don't see myself in the role of a great dissenter and I would much rather carry another mind even if it entails certain compromises," RBG said at a roundtable on judging in 1985. "Of course there is a question of bedrock principle where I won't compromise," she added, but she had "learned a lot about other minds paying attention to people's personalities in this job. I take that

As a federal appeals court judge in 1984

into account much more than just the ideas that I was dealing with in what I did before I came to the bench." RBG even tried to convince her fellow judges that when they all agreed on an opinion, they should leave off the name of the author entirely so the court could speak in a single voice. None of them liked that idea.

RBG's image as a moderate was clinched in March 1993, in a speech she gave at New York University known as the Madison Lecture. Sweeping judicial opinions, she told the audience, packed with many of her old New York friends, were counterproductive. Popular movements and legislatures had to first spur social change, or else there would be a backlash to the courts stepping in. As case in point, RBG chose an opinion that was very personal to plenty of people listening: *Roe v. Wade.*

The right had been aiming to overturn *Roe* for decades, and they'd gotten very close only months before the speech with *Planned Parenthood v. Casey*. Justices Anthony Kennedy, David Souter, and Sandra Day O'Connor had instead brokered a compromise, allowing states to put restrictions on abortion as long as they didn't pose an "undue burden" on women—or ban it before viability. Neither side was thrilled, but *Roe* was safe, at least for the moment. Just as feminists had caught their breath, RBG declared that *Roe* itself was the problem.

If only the court had acted more slowly, RBG said, and cut down one state law at a time the way she had gotten them to do with the jury and benefit cases. The justices could have been persuaded to build an architecture of women's equality that could house reproductive freedom. She said the very boldness of *Roe,* striking down all abortion bans until viability, had "halted a political process that was moving in a reform direction and thereby, I believe, prolonged divisiveness and deferred stable settlement of the issue."

This analysis remains controversial among historians, who say the political process of abortion access had stalled before *Roe*. Meanwhile, the record shows that there was no overnight eruption after *Roe*. In 1975, two years after the decision, no senator asked Supreme Court nominee John Paul Stevens about abortion. But Republicans, some of whom had been pro-choice, soon learned that being the anti-abortion party promised gains. And even if the court had taken another path, women's sexual liberation and autonomy might have still been profoundly unsettling. Still, RBG stuck to her guns, in the firm belief that lasting change is incremental.

For the feminists and lawyers listening to her Madison Lecture, RBG's argument felt like a betrayal. At dinner after the lecture, Burt Neuborne remembers, other feminists tore into their old friend. "They felt that *Roe* was so precarious, they were worried such an expression from Ruth would lead to it being overturned," he recalls. Not long afterward, when New York senator Daniel Patrick Moynihan suggested to Clinton that RBG be elevated to the Supreme Court, the president responded, "The women are against her." Ultimately, Erwin Griswold's speech, with its comparison to Thurgood Marshall, helped convince Clinton otherwise. It was almost enough for RBG to forgive Griswold for everything else.

A FULLY ADULT HUMAN,
RESPONSIBLE FOR HER OWN CHOICES

As word leaked out of Clinton's pick for the Court, the press struggled to figure RBG out. Was she some sort of flaming feminist? But what, then, explained her baffling D.C. Circuit record? A *Legal Times* study in 1988 found that RBG had voted with the famously conservative judge Robert Bork in 85 percent of the cases where they'd been on a panel together, compared with 38 percent of the time she voted with a fellow Carter appointee. And yet, six years earlier, when Ronald Reagan had nominated Bork to the Supreme Court, liberals had managed to get him tossed out of the running. (Senator Ted Kennedy had warned from the Senate floor that "Robert Bork's America is a land in which women would be forced into back-alley abortions" and where "blacks would sit at segregated lunch counters," among other horrors.)

BusinessWeek, at least, comforted its readers with the assurance of one Washington lawyer that the nominee "harbors no animosity towards Corporate America." *Chicago Tribune* columnist Clarence Page asked, "Is Ruth Bader Ginsburg another Thurgood Marshall or another Clarence Thomas?" He did concede that RBG was generally thought to be a "sweet lady." Harvard Law professor Alan Dershowitz, who had taught alongside Breyer, begged to differ. Cherry-picking anonymous reviews for his nationally syndicated column, Dershowitz said lawyers found her a "picky," "impatient," and "schoolmarmish" judge. (As of this writing, no one has come up with a male counterpart to "schoolmarmish.") Dershowitz claimed that RBG's "reputation among her colleagues—judges, law clerks and lawyers—is that she is a 'difficult person,' who alienates many of those around her."

Comparing RBG with Thurgood Marshall, said Dershowitz, was "denigrating the memory of a hero," because after all, she had only "argued a handful of appeals at a time when women's rights were voguish and certainly not career-threatening." Marshall had died five months earlier and could not be reached for comment. Another liberal lion and ally of RBG's high-court litigation, retired justice William Brennan, wrote RBG privately. "The president could not have made a better choice," wrote Brennan, by then nearing ninety. RBG replied, "Dear Bill, I love you! Pray for me, Ruth."

Now came what Clinton's staffers feared would be the hard part: getting a former feminist litigator and ACLU board member confirmed by the Senate. "Committee Republicans are looking for the letters that the President received on behalf of Ginsburg. They will not get same," wrote one Clinton administration official in notes from a meeting. "Rumor is that some abortion rights zealot in the White House advised Marty Ginsburg to start a campaign to overcome questions about her position on choice." In prep sessions, RBG was warned that she would be held accountable for anything the ACLU had ever done and was advised on how to distance herself. "I said, 'Stop, because I will not do anything to disparage the ACLU," RBG said later. "And so they grudgingly gave up."

At her confirmation hearings in 1993, RBG holds up her grandson's work.

In the end, in the four July days in which her nomination was considered, no one asked about the ACLU. The Senate was controlled by Democrats. After the pitched battles over Bork and Thomas, Republicans didn't seem to have much appetite for a fight. Two female senators had even joined the committee in the two years since Anita Hill, who had accused Thomas of sexual harassment, had been grilled by a panel of white males.

The country was introduced to RBG's slightly alien, flat cadence, stammering out two or three words at a time punctuated by perplexing silences in the middle of a sentence, as if she were reading aloud in a language not her own. RBG told charming and self-deprecating stories about her family, holding up a book made by Jane's son Paul called *My Grandma Is Very Special*. Senate Judiciary Committee chairman Joe Biden commented, "I will tell you, Paul, the handwriting is good, the pictures are beautiful and you don't need a publisher."

Her former client Stephen Wiesenfeld testified warmly on RBG's behalf, and Biden noted that he, like Wiesenfeld, had been a widowed father. And at Senator Ted Kennedy's prompting, RBG talked about some of the sexist slights she'd experienced over the years.

Strom Thurmond did press RBG on abortion. Wouldn't she agree that the judges in the *Casey* decision cared more about public opinion than what was legally right? RBG replied evenly, "I think that every justice of the Supreme Court and every federal judge would subscribe to the principle that a judge must do what he or she determines to be legally right."

"You are good, judge," Biden cackled. "You are real good."

Years later, during John Roberts's close-lipped confirmation hearings, Republicans would cite Ginsburg's careful answers to more pointed questions. "Time and again, she would say, 'I would apply the law to the facts of the case to the best of my abilities,'" remembered her clerk Alisa Klein, who sat in on the hearings. "Coming from some people that might be evasive. Anyone who knew her knows that she means what she said."

Eventually, conservative women rushed to testify before the Judiciary Committee to register their objections. One said that RBG had "demonstrated and spelled out her avowed devotion to privilege for females," showing "her tendency to be acutely aware of sex discrimination, not for males, but only for females." After all those years of being accused of advocating too much for the rights of men, RBG must have had a laugh about that one.

RBG did not apologize for the ACLU, for being a feminist, or for supporting abortion rights. "The decision whether or not to bear a child is central to a woman's life, to her well-being and dignity," she said simply. "It is a decision she must make for herself. When government controls that decision for her, she is being treated as less than a fully adult human responsible for her own choices."

When RBG's nomination reached the Senate floor, only three senators voted against her.

A GOOD DAY IN THE WORK OF THE COURT

As a new justice, RBG was now allowed into the room where once nine men had met to discuss the fate of the cases she'd argued decades before. She was part of the conference, where the justices shut the door and say what they really think. No one is allowed in this room but the justices themselves—"no secretary, no law clerk, not even a message-bearer," as RBG put it. Anything that comes out of that confidential meeting comes from one of them. The only record is handwritten notes, if the justices choose to take them.

A few days after oral argument, the justices meet for this conference to discuss the cases they've heard and take a vote. The chief justice sits at the head of one side, and the senior associate justice sits at the other. After the chief justice has summarized the case, the rest will speak their piece in order of seniority. There isn't much debate that happens in this room, according to RBG, despite the hope of outsiders that the justices might persuade one another at conference. "One justice or another will say, after we've talked for several minutes, 'It will all come out in the writing,'" RBG said. Then the chief justice assigns someone to write an opinion, unless he is in the minority, at which point the responsibility falls to the most senior justice in the majority.

RBG's first opinion as a Supreme Court justice was a dauntingly technical one. But three years into her tenure, she had a chance to finish something she had started decades before. Throughout the seventies, RBG had represented servicewomen in an ongoing bid to get brass to value their work equally. But the job of securing equality for women in the military was unfinished.

Another task was also incomplete. In her WRP years, RBG had never gotten the court to accept strict scrutiny for sex discrimination, the standard that would nearly write gendered categories out of the law. The women who wanted to attend a state's military academy helped her finish the job, this time as a justice. In the 1996 case of the Virginia Military Institute's refusal to admit women, RBG was happy to see that the federal government led the charge against the publicly funded school. For the litigator who had often faced down the federal government as an adversary, that was itself a victory.

VMI claimed that admitting women would undermine its mission, which included training cadets by an "adversative method" and which the academy argued couldn't be used to train women. After the federal government filed a discrimination claim, VMI set up a weak imitation at a sister school, which the state named the Virginia Women's Institute for Leadership.

With Chief Justice William Rehnquist in 1993

"What we have here is a single sex institution for men that's designed as a place to teach manly values that only men can learn, to show that men can suffer adversity and succeed, and a single sex institution for women that is openly, expressly, deliberately designed to teach to women womanly values, feminine values," said Deputy Solicitor General Paul Bender at oral argument. (It was the same Paul Bender who had heard Felix Frankfurter reject a female clerk.)

RBG had just one thing to add. "If women are to be leaders in life and in the military, then men have got to become accustomed to taking commands from women, and men won't become accustomed to that if women aren't let in," she said.

At conference, the vote, intoxicatingly, came down 7–1, with Justice Clarence Thomas recusing himself because he had a son at VMI and Scalia dissenting. The majority opinion was assigned to RBG. It would be her biggest victory yet. She could even approvingly cite cases she herself had won, and repudiate the bad old days, like when Myra Bradwell had been blocked from lawyering just because she was a woman.

FROM RBG'S OPINION IN *UNITED STATES V. VIRGINIA*

In 1971, for the first time in our Nation's history, this Court ruled in favor of a woman who complained that her State had denied her the equal protection of its laws. *Reed v. Reed* (holding unconstitutional Idaho Code prescription that, among "'several persons claiming and equally entitled to administer [a decedent's estate], males must be preferred to females'"). Since *Reed,* the Court has repeatedly recognized that **neither federal nor state government acts compatibly with the equal protection principle when a law or official policy denies to women, simply because they are women, full citizenship stature—equal opportunity to aspire, achieve, participate in and contribute to society based on their individual talents and capacities.**

Without equating gender classifications, for all purposes, to classifications based on race or national origin, the Court, **in post-*Reed* decisions, has carefully inspected official action that closes a door or denies opportunity to women (or to men).** . . . To summarize the Court's current directions for cases of official classification based on gender: Focusing on the differential treatment or denial of opportunity for which relief is sought, the reviewing court must determine whether the proffered justification is "exceedingly persuasive." The burden of justification is demanding and it rests entirely on the State. The State must show "at least that the [challenged] classification serves 'important governmental objectives and that the discriminatory means employed' are 'substantially related to the achievement of those objectives.'" . . . The justification must be genuine, not hypothesized or invented

As RBG has described her understanding of feminism, we must all be "free to be you and me."

RBG is happily citing her own successful legal strategy.

RBG is getting to cite her favorite Supreme Court case of widowed father Stephen Wiesenfeld.

This may be a comment on pregnancy, which the Supreme Court has never deemed to be discrimination based on sex.

RBG is always adamant to distinguish laws that target previously discriminated groups in order to remedy that discrimination from those that perpetuate historical inequality.

This is the case that said women were too delicate to tend bar unless their husband or father owned the place.

RBG is getting to set a new standard for laws that classify by sex, basically finishing the job she started in the 1970s.

RBG is laying her view of the Constitution, which she says is also "originalist": It's all there in the text; it's society that has to catch up.

post hoc in response to litigation. And it must not rely on overbroad generalizations about the different talents, capacities, or preferences of males and females. **See *Weinberger v. Wiesenfeld* (1975);** *Califano v. Goldfarb* (1977) (Stevens, J., concurring in judgment).

. . . **"Inherent differences" between men and women, we have come to appreciate, remain cause for celebration, but not for denigration of the members of either sex or for artificial constraints on an individual's opportunity.** Sex classifications may be used to compensate women "for particular economic disabilities [they have] suffered," **to "promot[e] equal employment opportunity, to advance full development of the talent and capacities of our Nation's people.** But such classifications may not be used, as they once were, **see *Goesaert,*** to create or perpetuate the legal, social, and economic inferiority of women.

. . . We conclude that Virginia has shown no **"exceedingly persuasive justification"** for excluding all women from the citizen soldier training afforded by VMI. . . .

A prime part of the history of our Constitution . . . is the story of the extension of constitutional rights and protections to people once ignored or excluded. **VMI's story continued as our comprehension of "We the People" expanded.**

In his dissent, Scalia said that the court had snuck in strict scrutiny through the back door. But nothing could temper RBG's joy. "I regard the VMI case as the culmination of the 1970s endeavor to open doors so that women could aspire and achieve without artificial constraints," she said. RBG sent a copy of her bench announcement to the ninety-year-old Justice Brennan, who had tried to get her five votes for strict scrutiny way back in *Frontiero*. She wrote, "Dear Bill, See how the light you shed has spread!"

On the day RBG read the opinion from the bench, a half dozen clerks were invited up to chambers to celebrate. There was no champagne, just an exultant justice. "It was the work of the court," said former clerk David Toscano, who was there. "It was a good day in the work of the court."

A little while later, RBG got a letter. It was from a 1967 graduate of VMI who said he was glad about the decision, because he knew young women who were tough enough to make it through. He even hoped his teenage daughter would consider it. A few months later, a second letter came from the same man. It was a bulkier envelope, with something tightly wrapped inside. As RBG unraveled it, she found a tiny tin soldier dangling from a pin. The letter writer's mother had just died, leaving behind a pin that had been presented to all of the mothers at her son's VMI graduation ceremony. He thought his mother would have wanted RBG to have it.

6

REAL LOVE

"I have been supportive of my wife since the beginning of time, and she has been supportive of me. It's not sacrifice; it's family."

—Marty Ginsburg, 1993

THIS IS THE STORY that Marty used to tell: After *Bush v. Gore,* and RBG's firm dissent, the two went to see the play *Proof* on Broadway. As they made their way back up the aisle for intermission, RBG unmistakable in her trademark scrunchie, the theater boomed with applause as people rose to their feet in appreciation. RBG couldn't help but smile.

That's when Marty, professor of tax law and inveterate joker, whispered loudly, "I bet you didn't know there was a convention of tax lawyers in town." RBG playfully smacked her husband in the stomach.

When Marty told this story in public, he would say it "fairly captures our nearly fifty-year happy marriage." It was a story that was about her, and people admiring her for standing up for what she believed in, but it was also about Marty—Marty being irreverent and funny, Marty being the opposite of the reserved RBG, and Marty bringing out a side of her that no one saw unless Marty was there.

It was hard to believe it happened, but clerk David Toscano saw with it his own two eyes in chambers: the justice jokingly chasing Marty around her desk with scissors. (The reason why has been lost to history.) He teased her publicly, about how the Supreme Court knew nothing about tax law, about her favorite snack of prunes, and she pretended to be put out. In his official

RBG hugs Marty during her ten-year Supreme Court law clerk reunion.

biography on his law firm's website, in words that could only have been Marty's, he was described as having "stood very low in his class and played on the golf team." Marty wore short-sleeved dress shirts and worn-out golf shirts, even sometimes around the office. He told everyone how his wife had made Law Review at Harvard and he hadn't.

With the same fondly amused grin he usually wore, Marty would portray himself as the lucky guy who came along for the ride of a lifetime, who moved to Washington when his wife got a "good job." It was a bit of a shtick. RBG, said her former clerk Margo Schlanger, "didn't have a husband the way many men have wives," meaning women who subsume themselves to their husband's careers. "The model was of equality, where they both were crazy superstars, in their own realms." Marty's tax law chops earned him clients like Ross Perot, the adulation of his peers, and millions of dollars.

So when RBG was asked how she had managed to have such an extraordinary marriage, she often answered by saying that Marty himself was extraordinary, and he saw the same in her. "He thought that I must be pretty good," RBG said, "because why would he decide that he wanted to spend his life with me?"

Toward the end of his life, Marty got a little more serious. According to Nina Totenberg, Marty told a friend, "I think that the most important thing I have done is enable Ruth to do what she has done."

MAKING PARTNER

At her confirmation hearings, RBG introduced Marty to the country with the phrase she had been using since the 1970s: her "life's partner." Each day, he would carry her briefcase into the Senate hearing room and spread out her papers on the desk. In Stephen Wiesenfeld's testimony at the hearings, he said he and his wife, like the Ginsburgs, had been "among the pioneers of alternative family lifestyles."

From the outside, neither Ginsburg seemed like anyone's version of "alternative." In New York, they had lived on the posh Upper East Side, on East Sixty-Ninth Street, and sent their children to Dalton and Brearley, private schools for the city's elite. Marty used to sardonically describe his work as having been "devoted to protecting the deservedly rich from the predations of the poor and downtrodden." On weekends, they golfed.

But if RBG hoped for a world in which men and women were freed of stereotypes, with full

At the Greenbrier resort circa 1972

and mutual participation at both work and home, she could look to her own enduring marriage as an example. It had sustained her even in the years where the answer elsewhere had always been no. "Fortunately, in my marriage, I didn't get second-class treatment," she said.

What Wiesenfeld meant by "alternative," and what was hinted by RBG's use of the phrase *life partner* was a marriage in which the woman didn't lose herself and her autonomy, in which two humans shared their lives and goals on equal footing. It wasn't so common anywhere, least of all among people who came of age in the 1950s.

Burt Neuborne, about a decade younger and married to another feminist attorney, remembers trying to tell Marty how much he tried to emulate him. "It was impossible to praise him, he wouldn't accept it. He shrugged it off. He turned it into a joke. 'You're not gonna blame that one on me.' I said, 'Marty, this is a new era, we all need role models.'"

RBG with her family at her swearing-in in 1993

In 1993, when the *New York Times* reported on the unusually active role Marty had taken in RBG's nomination, and the fact that he had over a decade earlier moved to Washington for her spot on the D.C. Circuit, Marty did not congratulate himself. "I have been supportive of my wife since the beginning of time," he said, "and she has been supportive of me. It's not sacrifice; it's family."

No one had been surprised that RBG had left Harvard for her husband's career. But she saw it as a give-and-take. "In the course of a marriage, one accommodates the other," RBG told me. "So, for example, when Marty was intent on becoming a partner in a New York law firm in five years, during that time, I was the major caretaker of our home and then child."

In Washington, RBG crashed her car into a gate, so Marty began driving his wife to the federal courthouse every day, until her Supreme Court appointment entitled her to her own car and driver. He read reams of books and told her which ones were worth taking a break from briefs. At parties, where she was inclined to hang back, he kept her moving around the room with gracious ease.

Marty often had to drag RBG out of the office. When she promised she would leave but hung on to do one more thing, Marty sometimes sang to her a line from Gilbert and Sullivan's *Pirates of Penzance*: "Yes, but you *don't* go!" Asked once if her husband ever gave her advice, RBG replied that the advice was generally for her to come home and eat dinner—he would start calling at seven thirty, and by nine she would have relented—and when she stayed up nights working, his advice was for her to go to sleep.

"Well, it's not that bad advice," Marty, sitting beside her, replied. "You have to eat one meal a day and you should go to sleep sometimes."

RBG paused to look at her husband lovingly, and then went on, "The principal advice that I have gotten from Marty throughout my life is that he always made me feel like I was better than I thought myself. I started out by being very unsure. Could I do this brief? Could I make this oral argument? To now where I am. I look at my colleagues and I say, 'It's a hard job, but I can do it at least as well as those guys.'"

CHEF SUPREME

Marty and RBG were lucky—they realized in retrospect—that soon after marrying, they got sent to a military base in Oklahoma. Spending almost two years away from everything they knew, Marty said, allowed the two "to learn about each other and begin to build a life."

For the first time in their lives, they had time. "I had a job that, quite literally, required my undivided attention four hours every week," Marty quipped of his army time. "You may as well just share jobs." That didn't necessarily mean splitting everything down the middle, but "doing whatever you did a little better or liked a little more or disliked less."

It turned out there was something Marty did a little better. It all started with tuna casserole, or at least something RBG called tuna casserole. At Fort Sill one night, right after they were married, she dutifully presented the dish. That was her job, after all, or one of them. Marty squinted at the lumpy mass. "What is it?" And then he taught himself how to cook.

Photograph by Mariana Cook made at the Ginsburgs' home in 1998

The Escoffier cookbook had been a wedding gift from RBG's cousin Richard. The legendary French chef had made his name at hotels like the Ritz in Paris and the Savoy in London. It was not exactly everyday fare for two young working parents on a military base in Oklahoma. But Marty found that his chemistry skills came in handy, and he began working his way through the book.

Still, for years, the daily cooking was still RBG's reluctant territory. Her repertoire involved thawing a frozen vegetable and some meat. "I had seven things I could make," RBG said, "and when we got to number seven, we went back to number one." Jane isn't sure she saw a fresh vegetable until she was sent to France the summer she turned fourteen. Around that time, she decided, as RBG put it to me, "that Mommy should be phased out of the kitchen altogether." RBG cooked her last meal in 1980.

The division of labor in the family, Jane would say, developed into this: "Mommy does the thinking and Daddy does the cooking." Growing up, James says, he got used to people asking him what his father did for a living, when his mother did something pretty interesting too.

In Washington, the Ginsburgs' shelves held more cookbooks than tax books. They filled three sets of shelves from floor to ceiling in the living room. Marty would consume cookbooks like they were mystery novels. "I hate Marty Ginsburg," Roger Wilkins, a friend of the couple's, once declared on a panel. "It's not because in a town known for its ephemeral passions, he's carrying on this lifelong love affair with this wonderful woman. It's because he cooks." In his house, Wilkins said, he was constantly asked, "Why can't you be like Marty?" Marty's recipes, joked another friend, were "the edible version of the Internal Revenue Code."

So RBG ate well. And slowly. Marty used to joke that it was a good thing Bill Clinton hadn't asked her to lunch at the White House, as he had asked Stephen Breyer, or else they'd still be eating.

JANE'S MOMMY WORKS

RBG had long known that pregnancy singled women out for unequal treatment. Parenting even more so. "What is very hard for most women is what happens when children are born," she said. "Will men become equal parents, sharing the joys as well as the burdens of bringing up the next generation? But that's my dream for the world, for every child to have two loving parents who share in raising the child."

Her friends say that's what she had, most of the time. Especially in the early years, when Jane was little. Having read that the first year of a child's life is when the personality is formed, Marty threw himself into caring for Jane while they were living in Oklahoma. He played classical music for her and took over the 2 A.M. feeding, because it was easier for him to fall back asleep.

Life in New York was another story. The mother of one of Jane's classmates at Brearley told her daughter to be extra nice to Jane, because, the woman said, pityingly, "Jane's mommy works." Marty was working to establish himself at his law firm, Weil Gotshal & Manges, and it was easy enough to fall into what was expected. True, the Ginsburgs agreed that unless there was something urgent, they would both be home by seven o'clock for dinner. Marty's firm was reputed to be "one of the biggest sweatshops in town," as RBG put it. But even without Marty putting in late nights, she said, "somehow the tax department flourished."

Still, falling into what was expected meant twice the burden for RBG, who was climbing the academic ladder while juggling care for baby James, born ten years after Jane. She had already gotten used to doing so much, but her patience with her husband wore thin. In 1969, she reportedly rebuked him, "Your son is now four years old and you've never taken him to the park." Marty said he looked back at it with some regret. "But it was also the way things were," he said.

Not forever. The balance shifted around the time RBG added the ACLU Women's Rights Project and Supreme Court advocacy to her docket. Teachers at the Dalton School had begun calling her constantly, complaining that James, then in elementary school, had gotten into trouble again. One day, he remembers, he snuck into the old-fashioned, pull-lever elevator unattended and took it up one flight—very much against the rules. Unluckily for him, the door opened right into the face of the janitor. When the school called his mother, she lost it.

"This child has two parents," she declared, asking them to alternate calls with her husband, starting with this one. RBG liked to say the calls decreased after that, because the school was loath to bother an important corporate attorney at work. James believes the calls tapered off because school administrators were so aghast at Marty's response to their description of the crime: "Your son stole the elevator!" "How far could he take it?" Marty replied.

In the late seventies, RBG was interviewed for a book called *Women Lawyers at Work*, which devoted many paragraphs to her work-life balance. The author, Elinor Porter Swiger, seemed eager to find her subject torn or in crisis. Swiger noted that Jane had once rebelliously announced she was going to be a stay-at-home mom like Evelyn Ginsburg. And Swiger pressed RBG for her reaction to a terrifying incident when James was two and a housekeeper found him screaming, with Drano on his lips. RBG vividly described rushing to the hospital: "Deep burns distorted his face, charred lips encircled his mouth—a tiny, burnt-out cavern ravaged by the lye." Swiger wondered: "How did Ruth feel during this prolonged ordeal? As a working mother, did she agonize with regret that she had not been there when it happened? The answer is a qualified 'yes.'" Then RBG paused to consider it. She said the real mistake had been "not putting the Drano out of the toddler's reach." Swiger wrote, not entirely admiringly, "It is a part of Ruth Ginsburg's success that she can view this incident in a relatively objective way."

As a parent, RBG could be "austere," as Jane put it. "When I did something bad, which happened often, my dad would yell, but my mother would be real quiet and I'd know she was very disappointed in me," Jane said. RBG went over her children's homework every day; one summer, James says, she gave her son the assignment of writing an essay every day. The kids tried to make her laugh, and a teenage Jane would write down each time she did so in a book called *Mommy Laughed*.

On vacation in the Virgin Islands in 1980

Still, the kids grew to appreciate what their mother was doing. In her high school yearbook, nearly a decade before RBG was even a judge, Jane listed her ambition "to see her mother appointed to the Supreme Court. If necessary, Jane will appoint her."

By the late seventies, Marty had had enough of working at his law firm full-time, and he had made his fortune. Having taught at NYU part-time for years, he accepted a job teaching tax law at Columbia Law School, where his wife taught (and where Jane would go on to teach, the first-ever mother-daughter professor pair at the school). A year after Marty settled in at Columbia, Carter's appointment of RBG to the D.C. Circuit meant Marty had to drop everything and move to Washington, where he began teaching at Georgetown University Law Center.

For years, people asked him if it was hard commuting back and forth between New York and Washington. It never occurred to them that a man would leave his job for his wife's career.

FIRST GENTLEMAN

Wives—and until 1981, they were always wives—of Supreme Court justices have historically had roles not unlike a gaggle of First Ladies: sitting for photographs in *Good Housekeeping,* sitting in a special reserved section of the court even after their husbands retired, gathering for lunch three times a year in what used to be called the Ladies Dining Room. When the second woman arrived on the court, it was conceded that this woman thing was probably not a fluke. In 1997, the room was finally renamed the Natalie Cornell Rehnquist Dining Room, after the chief justice's late wife. (It was Justice O'Connor's suggestion, and RBG sometimes pointed out that the Chief resisted change, but could not say no to that one.)

John O'Connor was the sole first gentleman for over a dozen years. He and Marty used to joke that they were members of the Dennis Thatcher Society, which Marty described as one's wife having "a job which deep in your heart you wish you had." Marty added, "Now let me just say that in my case it is not true. Only because I really don't like work. She works like fury all the time. The country's better off as it is."

In later years, when John O'Connor was diagnosed with Alzheimer's and Justice O'Connor retired, Marty was the only male member of the

En l'honneur de la Cour Suprême des États-Unis.

Le Vice-Président du Conseil d'État et Madame Marceau Long

prient Madame Ruth BADER-GINSBURG et Monsieur BADER-GINSBURG *de bien vouloir assister à la réception qu'ils donneront le Lundi 11 Juillet 1988 à 18 heures 30.*

R.S.V.P.   *40 20 80 04*

group. He didn't care, said Cathleen Douglas Stone, widow of William O. Douglas. "Marty liked being a spouse," she wrote in *Chef Supreme,* a cookbook of Marty's greatest hits put out by the Supreme Court Historical Society. "I remember being surprised when I realized his dishes weren't catered," she added.

On each clerk's birthday, Marty would bake a cake—almond or chocolate, sometimes ginger, lemon, or carrot. The justice would leave a to-the-point note: "It's your birthday, so Marty baked a cake." Sometimes the clerks would mull the day's work over Marty's biscotti.

"I was always in awe of her," says former clerk Kate Andrias, "but there was something disarming about seeing her with a partner who adores her but also treats her like a human being." Another clerk, Heather Elliott, wrote about one late night, after an event, when RBG was working in chambers while Marty read quietly. "I started to talk to her about the research I had done, and while I was talking, Marty got up and walked toward us. I started freaking out in my mind—'Is what I am saying that stupid? What is he coming over here for?!'—only to watch him come up to RBG, fix her collar (which had somehow fallen into disarray), and then go back to his book. The comfortable intimacy of that moment was something I will always remember."

RBG told me, "Marty was always my best friend."

That remarkable intimacy had survived Marty's bout with cancer in law school, and RBG's two diagnoses, a decade apart. Cancer had left them alone long enough to be together for the nearly sixty years they had been best friends. But it came back. In 2010, doctors said Marty had metastatic cancer.

"If my first memories are of Daddy cooking," Jane said, "so are my last. Cooking for Mother even when he could not himself eat, nor stand in the kitchen without pain, because for him it was ever a joy to discuss the law over dinner with Mother while ensuring that she ate well and with pleasure."

Before Marty's last trip to the hospital, RBG found a letter that he had left for her on a yellow pad by the bed.

6/17/10

My dearest Ruth —

You are the only person I have
loved in my life, setting aside, a bit,
parents and kids and their kids, and
I have admired and loved you
almost since the day we first
met at Cornell some 56 years ago.

nearly 60

What a treat it has been to
watch you progress to the very
top of the legal world!!

I will be in JH Medical Center until
Friday, June 25, I believe, and
between then and now I shall
think hard on my remaining health and
life, and whether on balance the
time has come for me to tough it out
or to take leave of life because
the loss of quality now simply overwhelms.
I hope you will support where I
come out, but I understand you may not.
I will not love you a jot less.

Marty

* 6/17/10 My dearest Ruth— You are the only person I have loved in my life, setting aside, a bit, parents and kids and their kids, and I have admired and loved you almost since the day we first met at Cornell some 56 years ago. What a treat it has been to watch you progress to the very top of the legal world!! I will be in JH Medical Center until Friday, June 25, I believe, and between then and now I shall think hard on my remaining health and life, and whether on balance the time has come for me to tough it out or to take leave of life because the loss of quality now simply overwhelms. I hope you will support where I come out, but I understand you may not. I will not love you a jot less. Marty

Marty died on June 27, within a week of their wedding anniversary and of the day RBG's mother had died. It was also the most important time of the Supreme Court calendar, the end of the term when all of the big decisions come down. The court was sitting the day after Marty's death, and RBG had an opinion in a key case, which said that a Christian group at a public university could not bar gay students from attending meetings.

Jane and James told her she had to show up in court; after all, she had never missed a day. "My father would certainly not have wanted her to miss the last days on the bench on account of his death," says Jane.

And so she sat there, very still, with a dark ribbon in her hair. As Chief Justice Roberts read a brief tribute to Marty, Scalia wept. Marty was buried at Arlington National Cemetery. Not long afterward, the folded American flag from his burial sat on the windowsill of RBG's chambers.

7

MY TEAM SUPREME

"She's Justice Ginsburg. I'm Justice O'Connor."

—Sandra Day O'Connor, 1997

WORKING FRIENDS

A buzzer rings five minutes before the justices take their seats at the bench, the closest thing the court comes to facing the public. They make their way to the Robing Room for a private ritual. Crossing the room, paneled in American quartered white oak, they approach lockers that bear their names written on gold plaques. Inside each locker is a black robe. RBG's chosen collar rests on an interior shelf.

Once robed, the justices shake hands with one another, before lining up in order of seniority and shuffling into the court chamber. RBG loves this tradition. To her, it enacts the collegiality that she has long treasured on the court. It is "a way of saying we are all in this together." So what if another justice responded to you, in RBG's memorable words, with a "spicy dissenting opinion"? The ideals of the court, of fairness and justice, transcend the daily tempers.

And yet. For years, something had been missing. If Sandra Day O'Connor, the first female justice and the only one for her first twelve years, had to go to the bathroom, she had to scurry back to her chambers. There was only

Justice Sonia Sotomayor
Appointed by Barack Obama
On the court since August 8, 2009
When Sotomayor was subjected to sexist and bigoted criticism shortly after her nomination, RBG spoke up on her behalf. "The notion that Sonia is an aggressive questioner—what else is new? Has anybody watched Scalia or Breyer up on the bench?" RBG said, adding, "She'll hold her own."

Justice Stephen Breyer
Appointed by Bill Clinton
On the court since August 3, 1994
RBG's fellow Carter and Clinton appointee tried to keep RBG awake at the last State of the Union— he and Kennedy "gave me a little jab, but it wasn't enough."

Justice Clarence Thomas
Appointed by George H. W. Bush
On the court since October 1991
Thomas calls RBG "a fabulous judge," and a friend, but they're ideological opposites. At his confirmation hearings, law professor Anita Hill accused Thomas of sexually harassing her. A copy of Hill's book Race, Gender, and Power in America was spotted on RBG's bookshelf in 1997.

Justice Antonin Scalia
Appointed by Ronald Reagan
On the court since September 26, 1986
Ever since their days serving on the D.C. Circuit together and despite their differing constitutional philosophies, "I have always enjoyed Nino," says RBG, using Scalia's nickname. When they're on the road, he's even her shopping buddy. Scalia says, "If you can't disagree ardently with your colleagues about some issues of law and yet personally still be friends, get another job, for Pete's sake."

Chief Justice John Roberts
Appointed by George W. Bush
On the court since September 2005
A familiar face from his arguments before the court, Roberts replaced Rehnquist, whom RBG still sometimes calls "my chief." RBG said in 2013, "I think the current Chief is very good at meeting and greeting people, always saying the right thing for the remarks he makes for five or ten minutes at various gatherings." RBG has said she hopes Roberts, like Rehnquist, might be teachable on the issues that matter to her.

JUSTICE ELENA KAGAN
Appointed by Barack Obama
On the court since August 7, 2010
Kagan laughs that when she graduated
from law school, the liberal judges on
the D.C. Circuit offered her clerkships,
but "the only one of President Carter's
nominees to the D.C. Circuit who
thought me not quite good enough
was Judge Ginsburg. She didn't even
interview me." This hasn't stopped them
from becoming close friends (or sharing
a personal trainer).

JUSTICE SAMUEL ALITO
Appointed by George W. Bush
On the court since January 31, 2006
In 2013, Alito rolled his eyes and made faces
in the courtroom while RBG read a dissent to
his opinion. "It was his natural reaction, but
probably if he could do it again, he would
have squelched it," RBG said charitably. It
bothers her more that the ultraconservative
Alito replaced the moderate O'Connor. "Every
5–4 decision when I was in the minority,
I would have been in the majority if she'd
stayed," RBG said in 2015.

JUSTICE ANTHONY KENNEDY
Appointed by Ronald Reagan
On the court since February 18, 1988
A fellow opera fan, Kennedy has appeared
onstage in productions in bit parts alongside
RBG and Scalia. But on the bench, he
infuriated RBG with his patronizing abortion
opinion in Gonzales v. Carhart.

a men's bathroom by the Robing Room. A second woman, RBG, had to join the court for it to get a women's bathroom. The renovation was, RBG said triumphantly, "a sign women were there to stay."

Two women on the court at once did not banish sexism. When RBG was first appointed to the court, the National Association of Women Judges presented her with "I'm Sandra" and "I'm Ruth" T-shirts. The white-bobbed

RBG and Sandra Day O'Connor in 2001

Arizonan and the dark-haired, bespectacled Brooklynite didn't look or sound anything alike. And yet, just as the trade group of female judges had predicted, based on their own years of experience, people constantly confused the two justices.

Even lawyers who should have known better. Arguing cases in 1997, for example, two repeat players before the court, Harvard Law professor Laurence Tribe and acting Solicitor General Walter Dellinger each flubbed the female justices' names. On the bench, O'Connor had to set the record straight: "She's Justice Ginsburg. I'm Justice O'Connor," she said firmly.

Of course, if either was *too* firm, she risked distinguishing herself in a different way. "Once Justice O'Connor was questioning counsel at oral argument," RBG recalled. "I thought she was done, so I asked a question, and Sandra said: 'Just a minute, I'm not finished.' So I apologized to her and she said, 'It's OK, Ruth. The guys do it to each other all the time, they step on each other's questions.' And then there appeared an item in *USA Today*, and the headline was something like 'Rude Ruth Interrupts Sandra.'"

RBG called O'Connor her "big sister." After all her years standing in for all women, O'Connor said of RBG, she "greeted her with enormous pleasure." When RBG fretted over the dry first opinion the chief justice assigned her, O'Connor gave her a pep talk. As RBG read that opinion on the bench, O'Connor, who had dissented in the case, passed her a note. "This is your first opinion for the Court," she had written. "It is a fine one, I look forward to many more." Remembering the comfort that note gave her on such a nerve-racking day, RBG did the same for the next two women to join the court, Sonia Sotomayor and Elena Kagan.

O'Connor and RBG shared a generation of firsts, women who had to be twice as good just to be given a shot. That was about all they had in common. A Republican party activist before she became a judge, O'Connor once gave speeches assuring wary men that unlike those flaming feminists, she came to them "wearing my bra and my wedding ring." RBG and O'Connor definitely didn't have jurisprudence in common either. A study found that in the decade they served together, O'Connor's votes diverged more from RBG's than from any other justice except John Paul Stevens. Even their disagreements pleased RBG, in a way: They proved women had diverse views. And unlike some of her fellow Reagan appointees, O'Connor had crossed the aisle in issues that affected women. The year before RBG joined the court, O'Connor, Kennedy, and Souter found a middle ground in *Planned Parenthood v. Casey* that saved the constitutional right to abortion. Every other year, RBG and O'Connor hosted dinners for the women in the Senate, back when there were only six.

Cancer invaded both women's lives. When RBG had colorectal surgery in 1999, O'Connor, who had survived breast cancer, was the one who gave her advice on scheduling chemotherapy for Fridays so she could recover over the weekend and be back on the bench the following Monday.

ODD COUPLES

RBG saw her fellow justices' reaction to her first cancer diagnosis as proof of the respectful, collegial environment of the court she so cherished. "Everyone rallied around me," she said. Even Chief Justice Rehnquist called her into his office and offered to "keep you light" on assignments, giving RBG her pick of opinions to write. (She didn't take him up on the offer to go easy, but did pick two opinions she wanted.)

Thirty years after being her biggest skeptic, Rehnquist had belatedly learned part of the feminist lesson RBG had tried to teach him. A 2002 case before the court, *Nevada Department of Human Resources v. Hibbs,* sounded like the next generation of Stephen Wiesenfeld, featuring a man needing unpaid time off to care for his sick wife. But this time, with RBG at his side, Rehnquist didn't crack jokes. He wrote an opinion citing RBG's Supreme Court litigation *and* her VMI opinion. "Stereotypes about women's domestic roles are reinforced by parallel stereotypes presuming a lack of domestic responsibilities for men," Rehnquist wrote. "Because employers continued to regard the family as the woman's domain, they often denied men similar accommodations or discouraged them from taking leave."

The opinion was so woven through with RBG's passions that Marty asked her if she had written it herself. RBG could fairly take a lot of credit for Rehnquist's evolution, but she gave him credit too. Her chief's life had changed after his daughter divorced. Rehnquist started leaving the court early to pick his granddaughters up from school. "Most people had no idea that there was that side to Rehnquist," RBG said. She learned it, serving beside him.

The least true image of RBG is the early Photoshop job that circulated online after *Bush v. Gore,* showing her with two middle fingers pointed upward and captioned "I dissent." Never happened, never will. No one is more committed to comity, to smiling through disagreement, than RBG. The proof is in the court's most famous odd-couple friendship.

It all started when Scalia, then a law professor, gave a speech fulminating about a decision by the D.C. Circuit court, on which they would soon both serve. Although the mild-mannered liberal RBG disagreed with the blustery conservative Scalia from the start, "I was fascinated by him because he was so intelligent and so amusing," RBG said. "You could still resist his position, but you just had to like him." By the time they were both on the Supreme Court, Scalia called her "an intelligent woman and a nice woman and a considerate woman—all the qualities that you like in a person."

Some liberals found the Scalia–Ginsburg friendship hard to grapple with. "At a holiday party last December to which Ginsburg friends of every stripe were invited," *Time* magazine reported when RBG was nominated, "Scalia came in and liberals edged to the opposite side of the room." During her confirmation hearings, some Democrats even fretted that RBG had somehow been influenced by Scalia's views. Even their clerks have been mystified by the relationship. But clerks work at the court for a year. For the justices, this is for life. Whatever their disagreements, they are stuck together. Besides, the two share a love of opera, and RBG likes people who can make her laugh. No wonder their unlikely friendship is now the subject of an opera, *Scalia/Ginsburg*.

For years, the Scalias and the Ginsburgs rang in the New Year together at the Ginsburg apartment, including some combination of Scalia's nine children and dozens of grandchildren. Scalia would bring the spoils of a recent hunting trip. "Scalia kills it and Marty cooks it," said guest and former Bush solicitor general Theodore Olson in 2007. "I never heard them talk about anything political or ideological, because there would be no point," RBG's grandson, Paul Spera, says. (Of the famous New Year's parties, Paul says, "It was really boring when you're a kid, all these old people dressed up for no reason.")

Inside RBG's chambers is a photograph of tiny RBG and rotund Scalia atop an elephant on a 1994 trip to India. "It was quite a magnificent, very elegant elephant," according to RBG. Her "feminist friends," she said, have asked why Scalia, a man, got to sit in the front. "It had to do with the distribution of weight," RBG deadpanned.

RBG and Antonin Scalia riding an elephant in India in 1994

RBG does sometimes let a little playful impatience slip. "I love him," she once said of Scalia, "but sometimes I'd like to strangle him." Her visible warmth toward Scalia doesn't extend to every single conservative justice. There are no reported opera outings with Justice Samuel Alito, though Alito has sometimes joined in the annual Shakespeare Theater mock trial RBG leads. Alito made it on the court despite a controversy over his membership in a conservative Princeton alumni group that objected to the inclusion of women and people of color on campus. There was no proof Alito had been an active member, and he disavowed the group in his hearings, but needless to say, he was no O'Connor.

Only one thing trumps RBG's commitment to keeping things civil at the court, and that is gently but firmly calling out sexism in the workplace. Even her own very high-profile workplace. When I asked her if she still experiences sexism, RBG replied readily. "Yes. Less than I once did. Once it happened all the time that I would say something and there was no response. And then a man would say the same thing and people would say, 'Good idea.'" She laughed. "That happens much less today."

Her response, she says, is to "try to teach through my opinions, through my speeches, how wrong it is to judge people on the basis of what they look like, color of their skin, whether they're men or women."

In 2009, President Barack Obama's nomination of Federal Appeals Court Judge Sonia Sotomayor relieved RBG of the unwelcome role of being the only woman on the court. The first Latina to be nominated, Sotomayor was promptly raked over the coals for a speech she had given in 2001. "I wonder whether by ignoring our differences as women or men of color we do a disservice both to the law and society," Sotomayor said in this speech, adding, "Justice O'Connor has often been cited as saying that a wise old man and wise old woman will reach the same conclusion in deciding cases. . . . I would hope that a wise Latina woman with the richness of her experiences would more often than not reach a better conclusion than a white male who hasn't lived that life." Republicans pounced. Conservative commentators began saying the woman who had been raised in a housing project and overcome so much adversity was the real racist.

RBG chose to enter the fray in unusually blunt terms, defending her future colleague before Sotomayor's nomination hearings had even begun. "I thought it was ridiculous for them to make a big deal out of that," she told *The New York Times Sunday Magazine*. RBG added, "I'm sure she meant no more than what I mean when I say: Yes, women bring a different life experience to the table. All of our differences make the conference better. That I'm a woman, that's part of it, that I'm Jewish, that's part of it, that I grew up in Brooklyn, N.Y., and I went to summer camp in the Adirondacks, all these things are part of me." As for Sotomayor's calling herself a product of affirmative action, RBG replied crisply, "So am I." It was an unmistakable gesture of solidarity toward another woman who would be a first.

Once Sotomayor was on the court, she was determined to stay true to herself. According to Joan Biskupic's book on Sotomayor, at the court's normally staid end-of-term party Sotomayor surprised everyone by putting on salsa music and cajoling the justices to dance with her. Marty Ginsburg had died only days earlier, and RBG sat quietly to the side. Sotomayor bent to whisper to RBG that Marty would have wanted her to dance. "Ginsburg relented and followed Sotomayor in a few steps," Biskupic wrote. "Ginsburg put her hands up to Sotomayor's face. Holding her two cheeks in her palms, Ginsburg said, 'Thank you.'"

The arrival of Elena Kagan as the fourth female justice marked the first time three women sat on the bench at once. RBG was elated. In 1973, in a move RBG hadn't even thought to attempt, the young Kagan had demanded her rabbi give her a female version of a bar mitzvah, then unheard-of at her Orthodox synagogue. As the first female dean of Harvard Law School, Ka-

"I'm gon' call my crew"

gan had recommended many of RBG's clerks. She was also the first woman to be confirmed as solicitor general. Still, Kagan acknowledged, her path had been much, much easier than RBG's. "Female law firm partners and law school professors weren't exactly the norm, but their numbers were growing, and they weren't thought of as tokens or curiosities," Kagan said of her earlier career. "Almost all federal judges and justices were happy to hire the brightest women as their clerks." (Kagan clerked for Thurgood Marshall.) "Although I won't say I never felt any bias, it was pretty easy for me to pick the path of my choosing," Kagan said, adding that she had RBG to thank: "More than any other person, she can take credit for making the law of this country work for women."

No one would be confusing the three women for one another. Her new colleagues, RBG said happily, are no "shrinking violets." For some reason, people repeatedly have asked RBG when she thought there would be enough women on the court. The question is asinine, her answer effective: "When there are nine."

RBG isn't a shrinking violet either. At oral argument, she has become known for often asking the first question. It is usually incisive, even if people have to strain to hear her. "Her tiny size and quiet voice—combined with the bad acoustics of the courtroom—can mislead visitors to argument into underestimating the justice," wrote Tom Goldstein, who frequently argues before the court. "It is not a mistake that the advocates make."

RED HOT PEN

It is writing an opinion, and the process of negotiating a position that at least five justices will agree to, that can often change the outcome of cases. "Sometimes in the process of stating your reasons, you begin to say, am I right? Did I overlook this question or that question?" RBG explained. "And not often, but sometimes, a justice will say, this opinion will not write. I was wrong at the conference; I'm going to take the other position."

After she circulates an opinion she has written, RBG said, she will sometimes get notes saying, "Dear Ruth, I might join your opinion if you change this, that, or the other thing." She usually agrees to the concessions, even if the result won't read exactly how it would if she were queen. "I try, even after I have the fifth vote, to accommodate a colleague," she said.

In her chambers in 2002

RBG, as the senior associate justice among the liberals, will often assign who writes the dissents. "I try to be fair, so no one ends up with all the dull cases while another has all the exciting cases," she told *The New Republic*. "I do take, I suppose, more than a fair share of the dissenting opinions in the most-watched cases."

Even a dissent doesn't necessarily mark game over. Occasionally, a dissenter's draft may be so persuasive that the majority flips. RBG pulled that off once, "a heady experience." A draft dissent might shame the majority into a narrower result. It might strengthen or focus the majority. Justice Scalia dropped his dissent in the VMI case in her lap on a Friday afternoon. RBG joked that he ruined her weekend but made her opinion better.

The night before RBG famously fell asleep at the State of the Union in 2015, she told me, "I thought to myself, 'Don't stay up all night,' but then my pen was hot." RBG's pen is often hot late at night.

Her clerks generally set their own hours and get their instructions from the justice through overnight voice mails. One night, former clerk Richard Primus remembers, he was working late and picked up the phone. "Richard, what are you doing there?" RBG said in surprise. The Supreme Court has an iron door that, at the time Samuel Bagenstos clerked, was locked at 2 A.M. "After that, the Supreme Court police has to be called to let you in and out," he recalled. During that 1997 term, he had to make that call repeatedly. "Kennedy is a morning person," remembers former clerk Daniel Rubens. "The joke was that he would see her on his way in and she was on her way out." No one has ever doubted RBG's work ethic. She used to be known for bringing a penlight to the movies to read her mail during previews, and to read briefs in the golf cart between strokes. As a child, her son would wake up in the middle of the night to find his mother scribbling away at legal pads spread across the dining room table, popping prunes.

Robert Cushman, the professor who made her realize what law could do in the world, told her early on that her writing was a little overwrought. RBG took a knife to her adjectives after that. "If my opinion runs more than twenty pages," she said, "I am disturbed that I couldn't do it shorter." The mantra in her chambers is "Get it right and keep it tight." She disdains legal Latin, and demands extra clarity in an opinion's opening lines, which she hopes the public will understand. "If you can say it in plain English, you should," RBG says. Going through "innumerable drafts," the goal is to write an opinion where no sentence should need to be read twice. "I think that law should be a literary profession," RBG says, "and the best legal practitioners regard law as an art as well as a craft."

RBG's clerks generally write memos on petitions to the court and are assigned to write the first drafts of opinions. They feverishly memorize the words they know she likes: *pathmarking,* a word she picked up in Sweden, and *because* (instead of *since)* for causality. Then they brace themselves for a brutal edit. Former clerk and onetime Columbia Law School dean David Schizer remembers another clerk showing him a draft opinion that RBG had gone over. She had crossed out and rewritten every single word in one paragraph—except "the," which she'd circled, in a move the clerk assumed was meant to spare his feelings.

RBG has been known to copyedit minor punctuation in a draft of a speech that was only going to be read, never published. There was a story that circulated among her clerks, possibly apocryphal, that RBG had sent a letter in reply to an applicant for a clerkship who'd made a typo in her application: "Note the typo." The candidate was not even interviewed. At the end of one term, her clerks presented RBG with the gift of a menu, edited in her fashion—nearly every word changed.

Schizer remembers a high compliment he got from RBG while clerking. He had just handed in a draft. "Marty wanted me to go to a movie and I said no," RBG told Schizer, evidently having set aside her whole evening to redo his draft. "But it's so good I'm going to the movies."

Grammatical correctness is the beginning, not the end of the story. RBG instructs her clerks always to remember that regular people are affected by the court's decisions and, if the draft is a majority opinion, always to treat the losing side respectfully. It sometimes reads like she is trying to defy anyone scanning for a stirring turn of phrase. "My writing style tends to be, some people might think, more bland," she said in 2012. "I'm not as immediately attention-grabbing, but I hope what I write has staying power." She often quotes Learned Hand—the same judge who refused to hire her because he didn't want to censor himself before a woman—that you shouldn't knock your opponent's chess pieces off the table.

"She had an acute sense of how the law intersected with real people's lives, and that both the actual rules but also the vocabulary you use to describe these rules also matter," former clerk Alisa Klein says. "The important takeaway for them is not just 'I lost.' It should be 'I was treated fairly and understand the judiciary.'" She also has instructed her clerks not to use the *courts below* or *lower courts* to describe the district and appeals courts, as an extra measure of respect.

Even with all this rigor, RBG's chambers are famous for getting opinions done fast. "We all laugh about how fast she is. And her work is just awesomely good," Kagan said. "In my book, she's the consummate judicial craftsman, and I learn something from her every time we sit."

A buzzer summons clerks to RBG's inner sanctum, where the granite-covered desk is often littered in chewed-up pencils. Most clerks came prepared to wait through what several of them called "her tolerance for conversation silence" but saw this as RBG choosing her spoken words as carefully as the words she writes. Richard Primus says he had the "Five Mississippi Rule," to know whether she was done speaking.

"There was always a point where you thought you were at the end of the conversation where you weren't sure if she was fully done," recalls former clerk Paul Berman. "You would slowly start backing up towards the door, and if she said something you'd come back, and if she didn't say anything you'd continue out the door."

HOW THE WORLD SHOULD BE

David Post had an asterisk on his résumé, for the two years in the eighties he had spent being a full-time dad. His wife was then traveling a lot for her job at the World Bank, so Post had stayed home with the kids during the day and gone to law school at Georgetown at night. He couldn't quite figure out how to describe that decision on his clerkship applications, and doesn't remember what terminology he settled on. Whatever it was, it caught RBG's eye.

"I wasn't the first guy in the world to do it but it was still pretty unusual," says Post of being the primary caregiver. He didn't realize then that RBG's favorite case was representing Stephen Wiesenfeld, who had been ready to take the lead in parenting even before his wife died. By the time Post was hired as a clerk for Judge Ginsburg at the D.C. Circuit, to begin in the fall of 1986, Post's daughter, Sarah, was about four, and his son, Sam, was a newborn. He mentioned that he would sometimes have to leave for day-care pickup, and RBG understood he would need to be home for dinner. In fact, she was thrilled by it.

"I thought, 'This is my dream of the way the world should be.' When fathers take equal responsibility for the care of their children, that's when women will truly be liberated," RBG explained in 1993 to the in-house paper at the Supreme Court. She had asked Post to come back to clerk for her in her first year as a justice. "I was so pleased to see that there are indeed men who are doing a parent's work, men who do not regard that as strange. People like David, I hope, will be role models for other men who may be fearful they won't succeed in their profession if they spend time caring for their children, or are concerned they will be thought of as less than a man if family is of prime importance."

Post later joked it was the best career move he had ever made. "Of course, a lot of women have to do it and no one made special efforts for them," he says.

Not long ago, after Post wrote a blog post about his experience, he got a note from RBG reminding him of something he had forgotten from almost thirty years earlier. The justice, an opera fan, had been pleased to see that Post's writing sample was about Wagner's Ring Cycle and contract law. Not much gets by RBG. "Ruth Ginsburg's a real pro," says Post. He'll never forget how, when his father was dying, the justice sent his parents a note saying they should be so proud of him.

In the eighteen months between their job interviews and when they began clerking for Judge Ginsburg on the D.C. Circuit, Susan and David Williams got married. "Justice Ginsburg was so delighted by this answer to the work/home conflict that she did some research to discover that we were, in her words, 'a Federal first'—the first co-clerks married before their employment began," the Williamses wrote.

One of the first things many clerks hear from RBG is that the most important job requirement is that they treat her two secretaries well. "There was one law clerk applicant who came to interview with me—top rating at Harvard—who treated my secretaries with disdain," RBG recalled. "As if they were just minions. So that is one very important thing—how you deal with my secretaries. They are not hired help. As I tell my clerks, 'if push came to shove, I could do your work—but I can't do without my secretaries.'"

Clerks were invited to the opera and to her home at the Watergate for dinner and a taste of Marty's cooking. And she seems to delight in learning more about the family lives of her clerks. When they have children, she sends them "RBG grandclerk" T-shirts with the Supreme Court seal.

When RBG heard through the grapevine that her clerk Paul Berman was dating a clerk for retired Justice Blackmun, Berman got buzzed by the intercom in chambers. He remembers picking up the phone apprehensively, thinking he had messed something up. "I didn't know you had a special friend at the court!" RBG cooed. "You must have her up for tea." Two days later, RBG had set up a small table in her chambers with a placemat and tea set, and spent thirty minutes with the young couple. Later, she performed their wedding ceremony, something she's done for several clerks.

"I'll never forget the end," says Berman. "Instead of 'by the power invested in me, by whatever' she said, 'by the power vested in me by the United States Constitution.' My wife always jokes that if we got divorced it would be unconstitutional."

RBG even occasionally gets in on clerk shenanigans. In Alito's first full term on the court, his clerks persuaded him to field his own fantasy baseball team along with the league the other justices' clerks had put together. "The week that the Ginsburg clerk teams played against Alito's, we beat him soundly," reports Scott Hershovitz, a clerk that year. Hershovitz eagerly reported the victory to RBG and suggested she send a memo to Alito crowing about the victory.

"She looked at me like I was crazy," he recalls. Hershovitz boldly slid a draft memo across the table.

RBG looked down at the page. "Now tell me what fantasy baseball is again?" she asked. She took out her pen to make some corrections. In the end, as Hershovitz remembers it, the memo read, "Dear Sam, I understand that this week my clerks beat your team by a score of 10 to nothing. We expect more, even from the junior justice."

8

YOUR WORDS JUST HYPNOTIZE ME

"Anyway, hope springs eternal. If I lose today,
there's hope that tomorrow will be better."

—RBG, 2012

RBG NEVER ESPECIALLY WANTED to be a great dissenter. She prefers not to lose, which is what, by definition, has happened to judges who write to dispute the court's majority opinion. Dissenters can leave clutching their dignity, gloriously unsullied by compromise. When Scalia dissents, he pours gasoline on the majority, lights a match, and stomps on the ashes. You can easily imagine his deep-throated chuckle to himself each time he crafts a zinger and calls the other justices' opinions "irrational" and "utter nonsense."

"I think when it's wrong," Scalia says, "it should be destroyed." But no one, probably least of all Supreme Court justices, changes her or his mind after being called an idiot. Actually changing the law means getting to five votes.

But sometimes, it's time to give up on persuading anyone else behind the scenes. It's time to get mad and let everyone else know about it. There are dissents that rose above their times, like in the *Dred Scott* case in 1857, when seven justices ruled that people of African descent were property and could never be citizens, or in 1896's *Plessy v. Ferguson*, where the majority upheld the doctrine of separate but equal. Those dissenters stopped speaking to their fellow justices and started speaking to the public, hoping the future would vindicate them.

The case that helped turn RBG into a great dissenter was one she never liked talking about. Few of the justices relished discussing *Bush v. Gore*, the surreal and bitter case that put the fate of the U.S. presidency in their hands. "It was described as a circus, but that is an insult to the discipline of circuses," said Theodore Olson, who represented then-Texas governor George W. Bush before the Supreme Court. And his side won. That fiasco culminated on December 12, 2000, with the court halting Florida's vote recount and effectively handing Bush the presidency.

The Supreme Court could have chosen to stay out of the Florida recount case and left it to the state courts, which is what RBG voted to do. Instead, the highest court hurried in twice. The second time, with everything at stake, the nine justices wrote six opinions. In an argument almost no one took seriously at the time and few have since, Kennedy and O'Connor's majority opinion said a recount would violate the Fourteenth Amendment's equal protection clause. It would supposedly "value one person's vote over that of another." The same words in the Constitution that had been used to desegregate schools, and which RBG had used to enshrine women's equality, were being used to shut down democracy.

There were four dissents. RBG's was calm and technical. "Federal courts defer to state high courts' interpretations of their state's own law," RBG wrote. "This principle reflects the core of federalism, on which all agree." Read closely, it very gently suggested the majority was being a bunch of arrogant hypocrites, who had checked their commitment to states' rights at the door when it served the Republican party. According to Jeffrey Toobin's *Too Close to Call*, RBG's dissent was initially a little less genteel, with a footnote alluding to the possible suppression of black voters in Florida—an actual equal protection violation. "The footnote sent Scalia into a rage, and he replied with a memo—in a sealed envelope, to be opened only by Ginsburg herself—accusing her of 'fouling our nest' and using 'Al Sharpton tactics,'" Toobin wrote. There was no such footnote in the final version.

RBG just wanted to move on. She later insisted that what she delicately referred to as the "December storm over the U.S. Supreme Court" was only a passing blight. "Whatever the tensions were that day," RBG said, it was time to come together and show that "all of us really do prize this institution more than our own egos."

RBG has never been very interested in drawing attention to herself without a good reason. That's how you know that when she does send up smoke signals, something has gone very wrong.

LONELY ON THE BENCH

In the span of three miserable months in 2005, RBG lost her friend Sandra Day O'Connor as a colleague and forever lost the man she would always fondly call "my chief." O'Connor announced in July she would retire at the relatively young age of seventy-five. She said she wanted to spend more time with her husband, who had been diagnosed with Alzheimer's. Then Rehnquist died of cancer on September 3, just before the new term was to begin.

President George W. Bush now had two vacancies to fill. He swiftly re-nominated the fifty-year-old John G. Roberts, his initial choice for O'Connor's seat, for chief justice. Replacing O'Connor would take longer. Bush hastily withdrew the nomination of White House counsel Harriet Miers, who was broadly considered unqualified. He settled on Appeals Court judge Samuel Alito. Suddenly, RBG was a member of a court that had just taken a sure step to the right, a triumph for conservatives that was decades in the making. They had seethed watching several Republican appointees, including Stevens, Souter, and O'Connor, turn out to be moderate jurists. With Bush's picks, the plan of conservative activists to undo what they saw as the excesses of the court in the sixties and seventies was back on track.

RBG was once again stuck in an all-male environment. At the dawn of the new term in the fall of 2006, TV newsman Mike Wallace reminded RBG in that in her confirmation hearings, she had said she expected to see three, four, or even more women on the court with her. "So, where are they?" he asked.

"Sadly they are not here," RBG replied bluntly. "Because the President has not nominated them and the Senate has not confirmed another woman. You would have to ask the political leaders why a woman was not chosen."

She had the same answer when asked by Linda Greenhouse of the *New York Times* about the fact that in that same term, the number of female clerks fell to single digits for the first time in more than a decade. Only seven women would be among the thirty-seven clerks, and two of them were working for RBG. Why not ask a justice who had hired no women? suggested RBG. That would be Alito, Souter, Scalia, and Thomas.

Her message was clear: The job of representing women should never have fallen to one woman. Being the only woman on the court brought

back grim memories of being something strange and singular at law school. History wasn't supposed to go backward, but once again, women were a "one-at-a-time curiosity, not the normal thing," in a place of power. That had damaging implications for all women. Girls wouldn't be able to imagine themselves on the court, and the diversity among women would be blotted out. Sharing the bench with O'Connor, RBG said in an interview in January 2007, had meant that people could look and say, "Here are two women. They don't look alike. They don't always vote alike. But here are two women." She added, in a rare moment of vulnerability—or maybe pointedness—"The word I would use to describe my position on the bench is 'lonely.'"

THE POOR LITTLE WOMAN

RBG joined the court feeling unusually optimistic about abortion. Only a year earlier, her new colleagues, in *Planned Parenthood v. Casey*, had reaffirmed the core of the abortion right recognized in *Roe v. Wade*. RBG thought that decision wasn't perfect, and that the restrictions it blessed would burden poor women. But it could have been worse, and at least *Casey* explicitly recognized women's rights and spoke about their equality: "The ability of women to participate equally in the economic and social life of the Nation has been facilitated by their ability to control their reproductive lives."

In 1993, RBG believed technology would take care of the rest of the conflict over abortion, thanks to newly approved pills that induced abortion early in pregnancy. "More and more I think that science is going to put this decision in women's hands," she said in an interview. "The law will become largely irrelevant." That's not at all what happened. Like almost everything else surrounding abortion, that medication became subject to a maze of restrictions blocking women's access to it. The right hadn't been able to ban abortion entirely, but it had found a way to make it ever harder to access, one seemingly benign regulation at a time. All this was seemingly enabled by the *Casey* decision, which said states could restrict abortion as long as they didn't put an "undue burden" on a woman's right to choose abortion. The law had stayed very much relevant.

Within three years of RBG's appointment, Bill Clinton, surrounded by women who had had tragic pregnancies, announced he would veto the so-called Partial-Birth Abortion Act. The law was pure demagoguery. There was a real abortion procedure some doctors used, rarely and later in pregnancy than the vast majority of abortions are performed, and banning it wouldn't change the number of abortions. It would, however, provide a platform for the anti-abortion movement to pelt America with gruesome images.

At former Chief Justice Rehnquist's funeral in 2005

Thwarted at the federal level, the movement went to sympathetic states to pass similar "partial-birth abortion" bans, which doctors protested were unconstitutional. "Whatever this particular ban does, it certainly can't be argued that it is passed in the interests of the health of the woman," RBG said at oral argument when the Supreme Court heard a challenge from a Nebraska doctor in *Stenberg v. Carhart*. In fact, the majority concluded the law made women *less* safe. "The State may promote but not endanger a woman's health when it regulates the methods of abortion," Breyer wrote for the majority, including O'Connor and Souter, striking down the law. RBG wrote separately to point out that the law was pointless on its own terms and to call it out for what it was: a long-term strategy to overturn *Roe*. Kennedy, who found the procedure grotesque, wrote a livid dissent.

All bets were off when George W. Bush triumphantly signed a new federal "partial-birth abortion" ban into law in 2003. Almost nothing in the law or the state of medical knowledge had changed since the court had rejected the concept the first time around. But the court as well as the presidency had. Back in 1992, in *Casey*, the plurality had agreed that Pennsylvania's law requiring women to notify their husbands they were having an abortion perpetuated traditional notions of male authority and would endanger women in abusive relationships. Only one lower court judge out of four who considered the spousal notification provision had deemed it constitutional. His name was Samuel Alito.

By the time the challenge to the federal "partial-birth abortion" ban reached the Supreme Court, in 2007, O'Connor was gone and Kennedy, as the remaining swing vote, controlled the court. And Kennedy was still angry about this particular abortion procedure. RBG had said the law did nothing to improve women's health or protect unborn life. Kennedy assumed it did. Writing for the majority in *Gonzales v. Carhart,* Kennedy gave voice to a new justification for abortion restrictions being pushed by the anti-abortion movement: protecting capricious women from themselves and from doctors who might lie to them.

"While we find no reliable data to measure the phenomenon," Kennedy wrote, "it seems unexceptionable to conclude some women come to regret their choice to abort the infant life they once created and sustained. Severe depression and loss of esteem can follow." By banning the procedure, if not all later abortions, Kennedy said he thought women might even be talked out of having an abortion altogether. Dahlia Lithwick wrote in *Slate* that Kennedy's "opinion blossoms from the premise that if all women were as sensitive as he is about the fundamental awfulness of this procedure, they'd all refuse to undergo it. Since they aren't, he'll decide for them."

Kennedy's opinion insulted RBG to her core. It undermined the work she had done to force the law to recognize women as fully and equally capable of charting their own destinies. Instead, it imagined "the poor little woman, to regret the choice that she made," as RBG later put it. In her dissent, which she summarized from the bench, RBG reminded Kennedy that his own decisions on abortion and gay rights had claimed that "our obligation is to define the liberty of all, not to mandate our own moral code." She even broke her rule of collegiality by noting icily that the court was "differently composed than it was when we last considered a restrictive abortion regulation," a not so veiled reference to Alito.

It was going to be a long term.

EXCERPT FROM RBG'S DISSENT IN *GONZALES V. CARHART*

The 1992 decision in *Planned Parenthood v. Casey*, coauthored by Kennedy, O'Connor, and Souter, affirmed a woman's right to end her pregnancy before the fetus was capable of living outside the womb, but said the state could pass restrictions that did not place an "undue burden" on her.

RBG is quoting from *Hoyt v. Florida*, the 1961 case about women being exempted from juries that was on her Women's Rights Project hit list.

Here, RBG is pointedly reminding Kennedy of the words he signed onto in *Casey*, from which he was now departing.

To RBG, abortion rights are about women's equality, not "privacy," a concept the court had slowly begun to recognize too. This is the most direct and sustained statement of this idea in a Supreme Court opinion.

As Casey comprehended, at stake in cases challenging abortion restrictions is a woman's **"control over her [own] destiny."** "There was a time, not so long ago," when women were **"regarded as the center of home and family life, with attendant special responsibilities that precluded full and independent legal status under the Constitution."**

Those views, this Court made clear in Casey, "are no longer consistent with our understanding of the family, the individual, or the Constitution." Women, it is now acknowledged, have the talent, capacity, and right "to participate equally in the economic and social life of the Nation." **Their ability to realize their full potential, the Court recognized, is intimately connected to "their ability to control their reproductive lives."** Thus, legal challenges to undue restrictions on abortion procedures do not seek to vindicate some generalized notion of privacy; **rather, they center on a woman's autonomy to determine her life's course, and thus to enjoy equal citizenship stature.**

Ultimately, the Court admits that "moral concerns" are at work, concerns that could yield prohibitions on any abortion. Notably, the concerns expressed are untethered to any ground genuinely serving the Government's interest in preserving life. By allowing such concerns to carry the day and case, overriding fundamental rights, the Court dishonors our precedent.

Revealing in this regard, the Court invokes an antiabortion shibboleth for which it concededly has no reliable evidence: **Women who have abortions come to regret their choices, and consequently suffer from "[s]evere depression and loss of esteem."** Because of women's fragile emotional state and because of the "bond of love the mother has for her child," the Court worries, doctors may withhold information about the nature of the intact D & E procedure. The solution the Court approves, then, is not to require doctors to inform women, accurately and adequately, of the different procedures and their attendant risks. Instead, the Court deprives women of the right to make an autonomous choice, even at the expense of their safety.

This way of thinking reflects ancient notions about women's place in the family and under the Constitution— ideas that have long since been discredited.

Though today's majority may regard women's feelings on the matter as "self-evident," this Court has repeatedly confirmed that "[t]he destiny of the woman must be shaped . . . on her own conception of her spiritual imperatives and her place in society."

. . . In sum, the notion that the Partial-Birth Abortion Ban Act furthers any legitimate governmental interest is, quite simply, irrational. The Court's defense of the statute provides no saving explanation. **In candor, the Act, and the Court's defense of it, cannot be understood as anything other than an effort to chip away at a right declared again and again by this Court—and with increasing comprehension of its centrality to women's lives.**

Unable to win majority support, over time anti-choice advocates began to justify restrictions on abortion as protecting women and not just the unborn. Kennedy's opinion reflects the influence of this new anti-abortion argument.

RBG is calling out the rationale for prohibiting abortion as "protecting women." She says that this kind of anti-abortion argument reflects and reinforces the very stereotypes about women's decision-making capacity and social roles that the court struck down as unconstitutional in sex discrimination cases— including in ones RBG argued herself. Once again, women are being told not to worry their pretty heads about it, this is for their own good.

There's no fooling RBG. She sees that the point of targeting so-called partial-birth abortions is to eventually go after all abortions the court protects.

COUNTED OUT AGAIN

Nothing prepared Lilly Ledbetter for the anonymous note left in her mailbox one evening, decades into working at the Goodyear Tire plant. Not the man who had told her he took orders from a bitch at home and wasn't about to take them from a bitch at work, or the boss who told her she could improve her evaluation by meeting him at the Ramada Inn. Ledbetter never found out who left the torn piece of paper with the tire room managers' salaries. The men each made around fifteen thousand dollars more than she did. That's when Ledbetter finally went to court.

By the time she was staring down the Corinthian columns of the Supreme Court, a federal appeals court had told Ledbetter she had waited too long to sue. Ledbetter's lawyers protested that each paycheck was itself an act of discrimination that restarted the clock.

At oral argument, Ledbetter had watched RBG, alone among the men of the bench. "We were around the same age, and she too had been one of the first women to break into her profession," Ledbetter later wrote. "I might have been on the factory floor as she walked the hallowed halls of the American justice system, but I imagined that men in ties and men in jeans can act just the same."

Unluckily, with O'Connor gone, business-friendly Alito got the majority opinion. He wrote, clinically and brusquely, that Ledbetter should have filed a charge of discrimination "within 180 days after each allegedly discriminatory employment decision was made and communicated to her."

As RBG read another dissent from the bench, it was clear that she felt the same kinship Ledbetter had. "It's the story of almost every working woman of her generation, which is close to mine," RBG later said. "She is in a job that has been done by men until she comes along. She gets the job, and she's encountering all kinds of flak. But she doesn't want to rock the boat." RBG was now in steady enough a position to rock that boat.

FROM RBG'S ORAL DISSENT IN *LEDBETTER V. GOODYEAR TIRE AND RUBBER COMPANY**

In our view, **the court does not comprehend or is indifferent to the insidious way in which women can be victims of pay discrimination.**

Today's decision counsels: **sue early on when it is uncertain whether discrimination accounts for the pay disparity you are beginning to experience.** Indeed, initially you may not know that men are receiving more for substantially similar work.

Of course, you are likely to lose such a less-than-fully-baked case.

If you sue only when the pay disparity becomes steady and large enough to enable you to mount a winnable case, you will be cut off at the court's threshold for suing too late. That **situation** cannot be what Congress intended when in Title VII it outlawed discrimination on the basis of race, color, religion, sex, or national origin in our nation's workplaces.

. . . Title VII was meant to govern real world employment practices and that world is what the court ignores today.

Comparative pay information is not routinely communicated to employees. **Instead it is often hidden from the employees' view.**

RBG was the only woman on the court at this time and was clearly trying to tell the other male justices that they have no clue what it's like to be a woman in the real world, working in a man's profession—like Lilly Ledbetter at Goodyear Tire and like Ruth Bader Ginsburg throughout her career.

Ironic coming from a court that has steadily made it clear that it wants fewer and fewer civil rights suits in the federal courts.

More real talk about how litigation works. It is almost impossible to successfully sue someone as soon as the first instance of discrimination occurs.

This refers to Title VII of the Civil Rights Act of 1964. The catch 22 effectively means no one could successfully sue for employment discrimination.

Pay disparities often occur, as they did in Ledbetter's case, in small increments. Only over time is there strong cause to suspect that discrimination is at work.

This is one of the employer's biggest advantages when it comes to pay equity. Imagine how the world of antidiscrimination law would be different if employee pay were public information, or, at least, open to other employees.

* Thanks to David S. Cohen, associate professor of law, Drexel University Thomas R. Kline School of Law, for help with commentary.

LILLY LEDBETTER: "Justice Ginsburg hit the nail on the head. . . . You can't expect people to go around asking their coworkers how much they are making. Plus, even if you know some people are getting paid a little more than you, that is no reason to suspect discrimination right away. Especially when you work at a place like I did, where you are the only woman in a male-dominated factory, you don't want to make waves unnecessarily. You want to try to fit in and get along."

Sounds a lot like RBG's own early life.

Damned if you do, damned if you don't—if she complains early on, she's labeled a troublemaker and suffers the consequences; if she waits, she loses her claim when she ultimately finds out there's been pay inequity that began a long time ago.

Each paycheck is a discrete act that employers are accountable for. As RBG sees it, if employers want secrecy, they need to be held responsible for what they hide.

Pay secrecy affects everyone, not just women under Title VII and, ultimately, not just with respect to unlawful discrimination.

Small initial discrepancies, even if the employee knows they exist, may not be seen as grounds for a federal case.

An employee like Ledbetter, trying to succeed in a male-dominated workplace, **in a job filled only by men before she was hired, understandably may be anxious to avoid making waves.**

. . . Ledbetter's initial readiness to give her employer the benefit of the doubt should not preclude her from later seeking redress for the continuing payment to her of a salary depressed because of her sex.

Yet, as the court reads Title VII, each and every pay decision Ledbetter did not properly challenge wiped the slate clean. Never mind the cumulative effect of a series of decisions that together set her pay well below that of every male Area Manager.

Knowingly carrying past pay discrimination forward must be treated as lawful.

Ledbetter may not be compensated under Title VII for the lower pay she was in fact receiving when she complained to the EEOC.

Notably, the same denial of relief would occur if Ledbetter encountered pay discrimination based on race, religion, age, national origin, or disability.

This is not the first time this court has ordered a cramped interpretation of Title VII, incompatible with the statute's broad remedial purpose.

In 1991, Congress passed a Civil Rights Act that effectively overruled several of this court's similarly restrictive decisions, including one on which the court relies today.

Today, the ball again lies in Congress's court. . . . The legislature has cause to note and to correct this court's parsimonious reading of Title VII.

This court has a history of getting Title VII wrong by not understanding that this law is supposed to help victims of discrimination, not hinder them.

The Democratic-controlled Congress picked up the ball that time, but by 2015, RBG told me, "The current Congress is not equipped really to do anything. So the kind of result that we got in the Ledbetter case is not easily achieved today. Someday, we will go back to having the kind of legislature that we should, where members, whatever party they belong to, want to make the thing work and cooperate with each other to see that that will happen."

Ginsburg: opinion in American Electric Power v. Conn.

Less than two years into its tenure, the supposedly consensus-seeking Roberts court was bitterly divided. Roberts himself was making his mark that 2006–2007 term by taking whacks at campaign-finance limits and by criticizing laws that tried to remedy racial discrimination for supposedly being racist in and of themselves. "The way to stop discrimination on the basis of race is to stop discriminating on the basis of race," Roberts declared in his majority opinion striking down a school desegregation plan. RBG joined the dissents in both cases.

RBG had never before read two dissents from the bench in one term, as she did with *Carhart* and *Ledbetter,* and people noticed. Cynthia Fuchs Epstein told the *New York Times,* "She has always been regarded as sort of a white-glove person, and she's achieved a lot that way. Now she is seeing that basic issues she's fought so hard for are in jeopardy, and she is less bound by what have been the conventions of the court." The piece was headlined "In Dissent, Ginsburg Finds Her Voice at Supreme Court." RBG joked that the news came as a surprise to Marty.

RBG made no apologies for the discord. At the end of that term, she warned in a speech, "I will continue to give voice to my dissent if, in my judgment, the court veers in the wrong direction when important matters are at stake." Metaphorically, at least, the gloves were off.

THEY HAVE NEVER BEEN A THIRTEEN-YEAR-OLD GIRL

The story of Lilly Ledbetter wasn't over. RBG had urged Congress to take up the cause, but she had to be patient. A bill to undo the majority's damage to antidiscrimination law died in a Republican Senate in 2008, and Bush had already said he would veto it. The election of Barack Obama changed that. Ten days into his presidency, Obama signed the Lilly Ledbetter Fair Pay Act into law, with Ledbetter beaming in red behind him. RBG put a framed copy of the law on her wall. Her ideal of a dialogue between the branches of government had been made reality.

Even so, RBG was still the only woman on the court, a struggle she found crossed ideological lines. That spring, the court heard oral argument in the case of thirteen-year-old Arizona student Savana Redding, who had been strip-searched at school because another student had claimed Redding had given her prescription-strength ibuprofen. The court had to decide whether strip-searching kids was constitutional, but that morning a few of the male justices—including at least one liberal—had trouble understanding what was so bad about what happened to Redding. "I'm trying to work out why is this a major thing to say strip down to your underclothes, which children do when they change for gym," Breyer mused. "In my experience when I was eight or ten or twelve years old, you know, we did take our clothes off once a day, we changed for gym, OK? And in my experience too, people did sometimes stick things in my underwear—" The court erupted in uncomfortable laughter. Thomas guffawed the loudest.

Breyer tried to recover. "Or not my underwear. Whatever. Whatever." By this point, he'd lost control of the room entirely. "I was the one who did it? I don't know. I mean, I don't think it's beyond human experience."

Redding was about the same age as RBG's granddaughter Clara. RBG had had enough. "It wasn't just that they were stripped to their underwear," she eventually snapped. "They were asked to shake their bra out—to shake, stretch the top of their pants, and shake that out."

Weeks later, David Souter announced his retirement, and RBG broke protocol. She wanted to talk about Savana Redding, even though the case hadn't yet been publicly decided. The debacle at oral argument, she told *USA Today,* was "just, for me, *Ledbetter* repeated." She meant the men on the court were completely divorced from women's daily realities. "They have never been a thirteen-year-old girl," RBG said of the other justices. "It's a very sensitive age for a girl. I didn't think that my colleagues, some of them, quite understood."

They didn't understand Savana Redding, and they didn't listen to Ruth Bader Ginsburg. "I don't know how many meetings I attended in the '60s and the '70s, where I would say something, and I thought it was a pretty good idea," RBG said. "Then somebody else would say exactly what I said. Then people would become alert to it, respond to it." Startlingly, the queen of collegiality now publicly accused her colleagues of repeating the bad old days. "It can happen even in the conferences in the court," RBG continued. "When I will say something—and I don't think I'm a confused speaker— and it isn't until somebody else says it that everyone will focus on the point."

That time, when RBG spoke, the men listened. On May 26, 2009, Obama nominated Sotomayor. And on June 25, the Court ruled unanimously that the school's strip-searching of Redding had been unconstitutional. RBG later told me she had changed her colleagues' minds. "As we live, we can learn," she said. "It's important to listen. So I'm very glad that case came out as it did."

A RAGING STORM

In 2006, Republicans and Democrats had come together to declare that even more than forty years after its passage, the Voting Rights Act was still necessary to protect minorities from disenfranchisement. A reauthorization of the 1965 legislation was unanimously approved in the Senate, passed 390–33 in the House, and signed into law by George W. Bush. However, this consensus hid a bubbling conservative rebellion. Decades earlier, a young Reagan administration lawyer named John Roberts had coauthored a memo arguing that the law should be written such that incidents of voter suppression would "not be too easy to prove, since they provide a basis for the most intrusive interference imaginable." Apparently it was harder for Roberts to imagine the intrusiveness of being blocked from voting.

At oral argument for *Shelby County v. Holder*, on February 27, 2013, Scalia had a theory for why the law had been so popular in Congress. "I think it is attributable, very likely attributable, to a phenomenon that is called perpetuation of racial entitlement," Scalia said. "It's been written about. Whenever a society adopts racial entitlements, it is very difficult to get out of them through the normal political processes." Black people, he implied, had wrested control of the government, and the poor politicians were too scared of looking racist to do anything about it. The court had to rescue them. In the lawyer's lounge of the court, people listening gasped aloud.

Conservatives talked a big game about the tyranny of unelected justices, but in *Shelby* the justices overrode elected officials to strike down a major portion of a law that helped people get access to the ballot. "The court has the reputation of being conservative, but if you take activism to mean readiness to strike down laws passed by Congress, I think the current court will go down in history as one of the most active courts in that regard," RBG told the *New York Times*. Her grim predictions have come true. In the years since *Shelby*, states have jumped to make it harder to vote, in a passel of laws whose impact falls disproportionately on people of color and the poor. "We put down the umbrella because we weren't getting wet," RBG said. "But the storm is raging."

FROM RBG'S DISSENT IN
*SHELBY COUNTY V. HOLDER**

RBG has vigorously defended voting rights since joining the court in 1993.

RBG is alluding to earlier federal civil rights statutes, local laws, and, most significantly, the fourteenth and fifteenth Amendments, which, even when combined, failed to prevent a century of voter discrimination.

As RBG notes, efforts to stamp out racial discrimination in voting were like a game of Whac-A-Mole, with new and inventive tactics deployed as soon as an existing one was outlawed.

It would be hard for RBG to overstate the importance and impact of the Voting Rights Act in transforming American democracy. Known as the "crown jewel" of the civil rights movement, Section 5 was at the heart of the VRA. As RBG notes later in her dissent, "Thanks to the Voting Rights Act, progress once the subject of a dream has been achieved and continues to be made."

* Thanks to Janai S. Nelson, associate director–counsel of the NAACP Legal Defense and Educational Fund for help with commentary.

"Voting discrimination still exists; no one doubts that." **But the Court today terminates the remedy that proved to be best suited to block that discrimination. The Voting Rights Act of 1965 (VRA) has worked to combat voting discrimination where other remedies had been tried and failed.** Particularly effective is the VRA's requirement of federal preclearance for all changes to voting laws in the regions of the country with the most aggravated records of rank discrimination against minority voting rights. A century after the Fourteenth and Fifteenth Amendments guaranteed citizens the right to vote free of discrimination on the basis of race, the "blight of racial discrimination in voting" continued to "infect the electoral process in parts of our country." Early attempts to cope with this vile infection resembled battling the Hydra. Whenever one form of voting discrimination was identified and prohibited, others sprang up in its place. **This Court repeatedly encountered the remarkable "variety and persistence" of laws disenfranchising minority citizens. . . .** Answering that need, **the Voting Rights Act became one of the most consequential, efficacious, and amply justified exercises of federal legislative power in our Nation's history.** Requiring federal preclearance of changes in voting laws in the covered jurisdictions—those States and localities where opposition to the Constitution's commands were most virulent—the

VRA provided a fit solution for minority voters as well as for States. Under the preclearance regime established by §5 of the VRA, covered jurisdictions must submit proposed changes in voting laws or procedures to the Department of Justice (DOJ), which has 60 days to respond to the changes. **A change will be approved unless DOJ finds it has "the purpose [or]... the effect of denying or abridging the right to vote on account of race or color." Ibid. In the alternative, the covered jurisdiction may seek approval by a three-judge District Court in the District of Columbia. . . . Congress approached the 2006 reauthorization of the VRA with great care and seriousness. The same cannot be said of the Court's opinion today.** The Court makes no genuine attempt to engage with the massive legislative record that Congress assembled. Instead, it relies on increases in voter registration and turnout as if that were the whole story. Without even identifying a standard of review, the Court dismissively brushes off arguments based on "data from the record," and declines to enter the "debat[e about] what [the] record shows." One would expect more from an opinion striking at the heart of the Nation's signal piece of civil-rights legislation. . . .

Leaping to resolve Shelby County's facial challenge without considering whether application of the VRA to Shelby County is constitutional, or even addressing the VRA's severability provision, the Court's opinion can hardly be described as an exemplar of restrained and moderate decision making. **Quite the opposite.** Hubris is a fit word for today's demolition of the VRA.

RBG is explaining the process of "preclearance." Effectively, certain jurisdictions, largely but not exclusively in the South, had managed to avoid the constitutional mandate to end racial discrimination in voting by inventing wily schemes to suppress the minority vote. Under preclearance, those jurisdictions were required to present all voting changes to either the U.S. Department of Justice or a federal trial court in D.C., in order to determine whether the proposal would put racial minorities in a worse position, before any change could go into effect.

Burn.

A facial challenge asserts that a law is always unconstitutional and should be struck down entirely, as opposed to a more narrow approach of declaring it unconstitutional as applied in a specific instance. Here, RBG is turning the tables on conservative members of the court and their supporters. They often wield the accusation of judicial activism at liberal judges and courts for allegedly overreaching in their decision making to address issues that are not properly before them. Here, RBG says to the conservative majority, "Slow down, love, please chill, drop the caper, you haven't even checked to see there's actual discrimination here or whether you can rule more narrowly."

. . . Volumes of evidence supported Congress' determination that the prospect of retrogression was real. **Throwing out preclearance when it has worked and is continuing to work to stop discriminatory changes is like throwing away your umbrella in a rainstorm because you are not getting wet. . . .**

The sad irony of today's decision lies in its utter failure to grasp why the VRA has proven effective. **The Court appears to believe that the VRA's success in eliminating the specific devices extant in 1965 means that preclearance is no longer needed. . . . With that belief, and the argument derived from it, history repeats itself.**

By June 2014, people knew to scan for "Ginsburg, J. filed a dissenting opinion." Five Republican-appointed male justices decided that not only did corporations have religious consciences, those consciences allowed them to opt out of covering birth control on their insurance plans. No big deal, said the majority in *Burwell v. Hobby Lobby*. Just ladies' stuff. Weeks later, when Katie Couric asked RBG, "Do you believe that the five male justices truly understood the ramifications of their decision?" she replied, "I would have to say no." Did they, as men, show a "blind spot"? Couric pressed. RBG said they did. "Contraceptive protection is something every woman must have access to, to control her own destiny," RBG said. "I certainly respect the belief of the Hobby Lobby owners. On the other hand, they have no constitutional right to foist that belief on the hundreds and hundreds of women who work for them who don't share that belief."

RBG's most famous words in the *Hobby Lobby* dissent could have appeared in any of her searing dissents: "The court, I fear, has ventured into a minefield."

Date Decided	Case	What Was at Stake
6/23/03	**Gratz v. Bollinger**	Is the University of Michigan's affirmative action program constitutional?
6/25/09	**Safford v. Redding**	Under what circumstances can school officials strip-search a thirteen-year-old girl?
6/29/09	**Ricci v. DiStefano**	Did the city of New Haven discriminate against white firefighter applicants when it threw out a test that had resulted in underrepresentation of black applicants?
1/21/10	**Citizens United v. Federal Election Commission**	How much can the government regulate corporate spending in elections?
3/29/11	**Connick v. Thompson**	Should a wrongfully convicted man on death row be awarded $14 million?
5/16/11	**Kentucky v. King**	What are the rights of a man whose apartment was searched for drugs?
6/20/11	**Walmart v. Dukes**	Can 1.5 million female Walmart workers sue for sex discrimination as a class?
3/20/12	**Coleman v. Maryland Court of Appeals**	Can state employees sue under a provision of the Family and Medical Leave Act?
6/28/12	**National Federation of Independent Business v. Sebelius**	Is requiring people to buy health insurance and states to expand Medicaid constitutional?
6/24/13	**Fisher v. University of Texas**	Is the University of Texas's affirmative action program constitutional?
6/24/13	**Vance v. Ball State University**	Who counts as your supervisor when they're harassing you at work?
6/30/14	**Burwell v. Hobby Lobby Stores, Inc.**	Can privately held corporations deny birth control coverage to employees if religious owners object to it?

"Such an untested prophecy should not decide the Presidency of the United States."

—RBG's *Bush v. Gore* dissent, December 12, 2000

DISSENTS

Result	RBG Says
No, because it gets too specific about its diversity goals and methods.	"Actions designed to burden groups long denied full citizenship stature are not sensibly ranked with measures taken to hasten the day when entrenched discrimination and its after effects have been extirpated," RBG wrote in her dissent.
RBG persuaded her colleagues that a search has to be "reasonably related to the objectives of the search and not excessively intrusive in light of the age and sex of the student and the nature of the infraction."	Her colleagues "have never been a thirteen-year-old girl. It's a very sensitive age for a girl. I didn't think that my colleagues, some of them, quite understood" (in an interview with *USA Today*).
Yes, in an 5–4 opinion by Kennedy.	RBG's dissent accused Kennedy of ignoring historical context and the facts, and declared, "The Court's order and opinion, I anticipate, will not have staying power."
Not much, according to a 5–4 opinion by Kennedy.	"If there was one decision I would overrule, it would be Citizens United," RBG told *The New Republic*. "I think the notion that we have all the democracy that money can buy strays so far from what our democracy is supposed to be."
A 5–4 opinion let the prosecutors off the hook	"It was an instance of extreme injustice. I thought that the court was not just wrong but egregiously so," RBG told *USA Today*.
The police won 8–1, in an opinion by Alito.	"The Court today arms the police with a way routinely to dishonor the Fourth Amendment's warrant requirement in drug cases," RBG wrote in her dissent.
Nope, in an opinion by Scalia.	"The plaintiffs' evidence, including class members' tales of their own experiences, suggests that gender bias suffused Wal-Mart's company culture" (in her partial dissent).
Nope, in a 5–4 opinion by Kennedy.	"The act was designed to promote women's opportunities to live balanced lives, at home and in gainful employment. . . . The Court's judgment dilutes the force of the Act and that is regrettable" (in her oral dissent).
Yes and no. The result technically didn't overturn the Affordable Care Act, but it upended precedent and, by making the Medicaid expansion optional, left millions uninsured.	"This rigid reading of the Commerce Clause makes scant sense and is stunningly retrogressive," RBG wrote in her partial dissent.
Maybe, said Justice Kennedy's opinion. It went back to the lower court, which let the policy stand.	"I have said before and reiterate here that only an ostrich could regard the supposedly neutral alternatives as race unconscious," RBG wrote.
In a 5–4 opinion by Alito, employers win.	The court, RBG said in her dissent, "ignores the conditions under which members of the work force labor, and disserves the objective of [civil rights law] to prevent discrimination from infecting the nation's workplaces."
Yes, in a 5–4 opinion by Alito.	"The exemption sought by Hobby Lobby and Conestoga would . . . deny legions of women who do not hold their employers' beliefs access to contraceptive coverage," she wrote in her dissent.

"The stain of generations of racial oppression is still visible in our society and the determination to hasten its removal remains vital."

—RBG's *Gratz v. Bollinger* dissent, June 23, 2003

9

I JUST LOVE YOUR
FLASHY WAYS

IRIN: *I heard you can do twenty push-ups.*

RBG: *Yes, but we do ten at a time. [Laughs.] And then I breathe for a bit, and do the second set.*

—MSNBC interview, 2015

A LOT OF PEOPLE throw around the word *unstoppable* when they talk about RBG. But they should know that it is literally true. Like the time the justice had a cracked rib, which wasn't about to stop her from keeping her twice-weekly personal training session.

Bryant Johnson has been her trainer for almost two decades. He tried telling her chambers that day in 2014 that he wasn't going to let RBG work out until her bone healed.

Johnson is sitting in his Washington, D.C., office as he tells the story, still incredulous. He remembers what her secretary told him in response: "She doesn't want to hear that."

It's not like Johnson isn't used to toughness. An army reserve sergeant first class, he used to jump out of helicopters and airplanes. He was deployed in Kuwait. He's also gotten accustomed to the kind of grit that comes in a power blazer rather than fatigues. Impressive professional women are basically his client specialty. But RBG is the one he calls TAN—tough as nails.

"I mean, she's not the heaviest or stoutest lady, but she's tough," says Johnson. "She works just as hard in the gym as she does on the bench."

RBG had always been thin, but after colorectal cancer, Marty started saying she looked like an Auschwitz survivor. He was the one who told her in 1999 she had to see a trainer, along with Sandra Day O'Connor, who had advised RBG to stay active during cancer. (Being a night person, RBG never made it to O'Connor's 8 A.M. aerobics class, which O'Connor had basically required female clerks to attend.) At twenty-nine, RBG discovered the Canadian Air Force workout at a tax conference with Marty, and she has performed it almost daily since. Designed in the 1950s, its moves include quick spurts of toe-touching, knee-raising, arm-circling, and leg-lifting.

For most of her life, people have thought of RBG as formal, cold even. But there was another, less guarded side, the one that came out as when she threw herself into horseback riding or waterskiing. One summer when

White-water rafting in Colorado in 1990

they were both teaching in Aspen, Colorado, Burt Neuborne, RBG, and a few other friends went whitewater rafting on the Colorado River. RBG was pushing sixty, and she had never been a large woman. "I told Ruth she should sit in the back of the boat, because she was so light that if they hit a rock, she would go flying over," Neuborne says. "Her response: 'I don't sit in the back.'" A few years later, a friend recruited by Marty to lobby for RBG's nomination to the court, N. Jerold Cohen, said, "Early on it came out that President Clinton was looking for a young jurist, and I pointed out that she's in great physical shape." In residence for a week at the University of Hawaii in 1998, already a justice, RBG gleefully went paddleboarding.

When RBG and O'Connor gave the U.S. Olympic Women's Basketball team a tour of the court, including the "highest court in the land," the basketball court upstairs, RBG gamely agreed to take a shot. A little practice, the players agreed, and she could be a point guard. At her seventy-fifth birthday celebration at the Second Circuit, the Court of Appeals she oversees, RBG was asked whom she wanted to record a birthday greeting for her to be played on a screen. She surprised everyone by picking legendary Yankees manager Joe Torre.

After massive surgery, chemotherapy, and radiation—"the whole works," RBG conceded—it was time to rebuild. Her friend Gladys Kessler, a federal judge in Washington, D.C., had a recommendation for her: Johnson, whose day job was in Kessler's office as a records manager. Johnson didn't quite know what RBG had been through, but he didn't really care. He would meet her where she was and go from there. And RBG took to strength training like she does everything else: with ferocious determination, and without complaint.

"She uses her mind every day," says Johnson, "and I make sure she uses her body."

He started with having her do push-ups on the wall, feet on the ground. RBG said skeptically, "Push-ups?" And Johnson replied, *"Yes, push-ups."*

In their first few months of training, Johnson was worried that he hadn't gotten any feedback from RBG. "If the justice didn't like you," one of her secretaries told him, "you wouldn't still be here." He didn't ask that question again.

Johnson still has the broad shoulders and iron posture of a military man, but he likes to wear blue-tinted glasses and answer e-mails with "kool and the gang." Johnson comes across as a man who is used to making awkward, cerebral people feel comfortable, which is to say he is comfortable with himself. He cracks jokes and says RBG even laughs at them, despite her old rep, including with her kids, for not having a sense of humor.

There's a competition happening in his office for floor space, between boxes of yellowed archival documents and duffel bags of exercise equipment. On the corner shelf sits a "Notorious RBG" T-shirt along with an "I <3 RBG" hat, both gifts from his most famous client. A half-unzipped black bag under his desk reveals a pair of boxing gloves that are usually used by his second most famous client, Justice Elena Kagan—who came to him on RBG's recommendation.

He gets these women, how they have had to barrel fearlessly—but not too hard—through the world. "Being a woman in this city, you've got to be able to put up with a little bit and be able to take a lot of it," he says. "You're looking at Justice Ginsburg, Judge Kessler, these are women that when they came through, they were told, 'You want to be a lawyer? You can be a paralegal, you can't be a lawyer.'"

Still on reserve duty, Johnson also works on sexual-assault prevention and victim advocacy, helping service members who have filed sexual-assault complaints know their options and seeing them through the process. Does he call himself a feminist? "I have been raised with a lot of strong women in my life that help influence how I look at women," he says, "which is as equal to a man." (He hastens to add his grandmother taught him to always open doors for women.)

After the wall push-ups came push-ups on her knees. After that, push-ups with knees off the ground. That was when, Johnson gloats, "I could see the light in her eyes." Sometimes she'll go over twenty. Sometimes he has to protect her from herself on that too.

Johnson was never one of the people who saw RBG's birdlike build or her postcancer pallor and thought that was it. A few years ago, *The New Yorker*'s Jeffrey Toobin, who described RBG as "frail" in one of his books on the court, learned the error of his ways in a pretty direct fashion. As in, Marty in his face, asking him, "How many push-ups can you do?"

As Toobin struggled to come up with a number, Marty retorted, "My wife can do twenty-five—and you wrote that she was 'frail.'"

Bryant Johnson still gets asked if the justice actually does "girl push-ups," with her knees down. He rejects that term (and anyway, she doesn't). "A push-up is a push-up is a push-up," he says. "I don't look at the fact that they're a woman by limiting what they can do."

That's not to say he doesn't see *any* difference between men and women at the gym. In fact, he sees some right inside the special, justices-only gym where he trains RBG. "I've seen the Chief there, and Justice Breyer," Johnson says.

He rolls his eyes. "Men, we have that ego thing: 'Yeah, I know how to do it. I know how to lift weights, I know how to work on a car.' Women understand, 'Yeah, I don't know how to lift weights,'" he says. "Justice Ginsburg knows about the law, but when it comes to personal training, I explain it to you."

The only thing she tries to explain to him is opera. "Sometimes I understand it," confesses Johnson. "Sometimes I'm like . . . *yeah*. That's her thing." Before there was a television in the justices' gym, RBG would work out to classical music. (A Jazzercise class she attended in the early nineties, she told *The New Republic* in horror, "was accompanied by loud music, sounding quite awful to me.")

Now, PBS's *NewsHour* is usually on while they train. "I even became a fan of *NewsHour*," Johnson says, not exactly with enthusiasm. He was pretty relieved the first time Kagan asked to flip to ESPN's *SportsCenter* for her own gym time.

And he was thrilled to teach Kagan how to box. "How many women know how to punch? It's not a ladylike thing," says Johnson. "But there's nothing like the sound of leather hitting leather. When you hear that pop sound"—he mimes a punch and makes the sound *buh, buh, buh*—"that's a feeling that sometimes women don't get." He's even created an extended boxing sequence he calls the "Kagan combination."

One evening—and her training sessions are almost always in the evening, usually at 7 P.M.—when RBG's session directly followed Kagan's, she asked about those gloves. Johnson suggested the senior justice give them a thump. "She said, 'No, we'll leave that for her.'"

So had RBG finally found her limit?

Johnson has a theory about that: "She's already empowered."

If he wanted to, Johnson could take some credit for the fact that RBG has kept up her daunting work output and her frenetic social schedule past the age of eighty. Mostly he's just happy that, he says, RBG hasn't lost any bone density since they began training, which beats the odds for her age. "She fell in her chambers once, on her hip," he said. "What happens to older women when they fall?" Johnson was referring to the fact that they often break bones. "She went to the doctor, came back, and said, 'Nothing's broken.' That was my report card."

They had a scare during one training session, when RBG started feeling light-headed. Her chest felt constricted, and she broke out in a sweat. She wondered whether it was because she had stayed up the night before writing an opinion, and wanted to ignore it. "I was very stubborn," she says. Johnson called her secretary, who, as RBG puts it, in her "gently persuasive way," insisted she go to the hospital.

As Johnson saw RBG to the ambulance, he promised, "You ain't going out on my watch." He added something else that made RBG smile: "I said, 'Justice, you do realize this is not going to get you out of doing these push-ups.'"

An EKG showed she had a blocked right coronary artery, and doctors put in a stent. "I was fine," RBG told me. "No more constriction in my chest. I wanted to go home." She laughed. The doctors insisted she stay in the hospital two nights.

When her hospital stay became public, Johnson got a text message from a fellow trainer in Ohio, whom he'd met at a fitness convention, where RBG was an instant hero. "'Yo B, what you doing to the justice, man?'" his friend demanded. "I'm like, 'How do you know?' 'We keep NPR on!'"

The heart stent was inserted on a Wednesday. RBG still wanted to train on the following Monday. That time, Johnson relented—as long as they only did stretching exercises. By then, he knew she would pick working out over almost anything else. Even her own bones. Even dinner with the president.

RBG plainly adores Barack Obama. She calls him *"sympathique,"* a French word that is one of her highest forms of praise. And yet one night, Johnson remembers, RBG slipped out early from a dinner at the White House. After all, she had a date at the gym.

"I said, 'You left the president for me?'" Johnson recalls. "'Oh man, extra push-ups for you.'"

THE NOTORIOUS RBG WORKOUT

The justice starts with a five-minute warm-up on the elliptical, followed by stretching and rotational exercises. Lately, Bryant Johnson has had her do one-legged squats—holding on to his hands—and planks, where he does his best to knock the tiny justice down. But the signature move is one that Johnson describes as "the exercise that will actually stop you from having to have a nurse 24/7," preventing the client from getting to "the moment you can't sit down at the toilet and get up."

1. Sit down on a bench with a 12-pound ball. (RBG started with a 2-pound ball and made her way up. "The first time I gave her the 12-pound ball, it almost threw her," Johnson says.)

2. Stand up, holding the ball with two hands; press it to your chest.

3. Toss it to Johnson, who hands it back. ("I don't want to take the chance she misses it and it hits her. That wouldn't be a good look. Just think of the paperwork I would have to fill out.")

4. Sit back down on the bench.

5. Repeat 10 times.

RBG'S SWAG

Among rows of black robes, in a city of sensible conformity, RBG has boldly staked out her own aesthetic. Like everything else about RBG, it is precise, elegant, and at times unexpectedly audacious. And every detail matters—not just because she's a perfectionist, although she is, but because it tells a story.

The lacy collar, or jabot, the visual she is most known for—a glimpse into the closet in her chambers shows she has at least a dozen—started out as a quietly political statement about women on the bench. "You know, the standard robe is made for a man because it has a place for the shirt to show, and the tie," RBG said. "So Sandra Day O'Connor and I thought it would

be appropriate if we included as part of our robe something typical of a woman. So I have many, many collars." She and O'Connor took something that had never been made with a woman in mind, because no one ever imagined the world other than how it was, and they made it theirs.

Male justices gussied up too. Rehnquist added gold stripes to his robes in a nod to Gilbert and Sullivan's *Iolanthe*. (RBG, a huge Gilbert and Sullivan fan herself, once jokingly presented him with a white English-style wig.) And John Paul Stevens had his trademark bow ties.

But RBG's jabots are a language of their own. The justice who despises frippery in her writing uses her neck accessories as a rhetorical flourish. The glass-beaded velvet bib necklace she wears to dissent is made by Banana Republic, obtained from a gift bag when she was one of *Glamour*'s Women of the Year in 2012. "It looks fitting for dissent," she said simply.

RBG's majority-opinion jabot—not seen too

often these days—dangles with gold trim and charms. It was a gift from her law clerks. One of her favorites, a uniform crocheted white ring, was first spotted in a museum in Cape Town, South Africa. Another was purchased in the gift shop of the Metropolitan Opera, a two-pronged copy of the collar worn by one of her favorite tenors, Placido Domingo, in Verdi's *Stiffelio*. That reminded RBG of what she called one of the best days of her life, when Domingo surprised her by serenading her as they both received honorary degrees from Harvard. Her favorite tenor, *and* it was belated justice a half century after the dean of the law school had denied her a Harvard degree, all in a day. "It was glorious," she said.

So far, however, her efforts to pass on the collar habit to the younger generation have stalled. At the Supreme Court, justices are sworn in twice, the second time publicly in a formal proceeding known as an investiture. At Sotomayor's 2009 ceremony, the newest justice wore a jabot that encircled her neck with a row of lace, culminating in two lace blossoms and a flap of plain starched white down the center. It was a gift from Justice Ginsburg, reporters were told. But judging from court sketches and official portraits, it didn't last. Sotomayor is generally spotted in her trademark dangly earrings paired with an unadorned robe.

Kagan was already a good friend of RBG's when she joined the court, but she drew a firm sartorial line from the start. "I think you just have to do what makes you feel comfortable," Kagan said not long into her tenure. "In my real life I'm not a frilly, lacy person. Some of the things people wear just struck me as not something I felt comfortable with." RBG did not hold it against her.

If the jabot is RBG's mark of individuality, every justice's robe is meant to signal a kind of uniformity. "It's, I think, a symbol of 'we are all in the business of impartial judging,'" RBG said of the black cloaking. "And in the United

States I think the pattern was set by the great Chief Justice John Marshall, who said that judges in the United States should not wear royal robes. They should not wear red robes or maroon robes. They should wear plain black."

At the time, though, Marshall assumed an all-male bench. "I didn't know anyone who made robes for women justices," said O'Connor, who bore the burden of being the first female justice. "Most of what was available was something like a choir robe or an academic robe." RBG's usual robe is from England, a Lord Mayor's robe she likes. Off the bench, when she judges mock trials, she occasionally allows herself a little more pomp. As a guest in China in the nineties, she admired the judges' red and black robes and was eventually given one as a gift.

"The judiciary is not a profession that ranks very high among the glamorously attired," RBG declared from the hallowed stage of Carnegie Hall at *Glamour*'s Women of the Year event. But RBG herself is an exception. She's long been a dark-horse darling of the glossies. Her outfits at her confirmation hearing earned praise in *The New York Times Magazine* from none other than legendary fashion editor Carrie Donovan, formerly of *Vogue* and *Harper's Bazaar*. "When she turned up at the Senate last summer in a swingy pleated skirt and striped tunic-length top with a string of beads, she looked more pulled together than any woman in the Washington eye since Jackie Kennedy Onassis," Donovan wrote.

Writing about a visit to RBG's chambers in the same magazine in 1997, Jeffrey Rosen also compared her aplomb with Jackie O and her famous televised White House tour, and then offered this unusual rhapsody: "It was hard not to be struck by her improbable glamour. Scarcely more than five feet tall, in a turquoise Chinese-silk jacket with matching wide-legged pants, her black hair pulled tightly back in a ponytail, she looked like an exquisite figurine." A secretary at Marty's law firm in New York who became a feminist after typing up RBG's briefs for her remembered being flummoxed when the lady lawyer appeared in a green dashiki, looking nothing like the secretary had imagined.

These days, RBG favors regal, loosely fitting robes of brocades or embroidered silks, usually accented with statement jewelry: ropes of pearls, a single string of red she has been wearing for decades, or a large pendant.

She doesn't have her ears pierced but often wears prominent colored stud or dangling earrings. RBG often picks things up when she's traveling. David Schizer remembers her jokingly complaining that because Marty wasn't much of a shopper, Nino—that would be Justice Antonin Scalia—would go with her instead.

With then-Senator Joe Biden in 1993

Rarely does she go casual. According to Jeffrey Toobin's *The Nine,* during a massive snowstorm, RBG and the other justices were picked up in jeeps for oral argument. "Ginsburg chose to wear a straight skirt and high heels," Toobin reported. "Because of the snow on the ground and Ginsburg's outfit, the driver, who usually worked in the clerk's office, had to lift the tiny justice into the air and deposit her in the car. (Later, Ginsburg wrote the fellow a letter of recommendation for law school.)"

Dress is one issue on which RBG can be a conservative. Her oldest granddaughter, Clara, says RBG will not-so-subtly offer her a shawl if she thinks Clara's shirt is too low cut. In her freshman year of college, Clara got her nose pierced, along with a total of thirteen piercings in her ears, much to RBG's horror. "She kept calling it 'that thing on your face,'" Clara says, amused. To me, RBG expressed relief that at least a nose ring, unlike a tattoo, could be easily removed.

At public functions, RBG wears gloves, often black or white lace. In the dead of winter in Michigan, she wore daring knee-high leather boots. She usually carries the Constitution in her handbag, and after she got an MZ Wallace tote in the *Glamour* gift bag, she liked it so much she bought another.

(She bought one for Clara too.) She has a weakness for Ferragamo shoes. RBG's hair is invariably combed back severely, often affixed with a scrunchie. Every once in a while, she would come to chambers wearing a turban, and

And then I meet Ruth Bader Ginsburg. She is PETITE and Elegant. I think, move over Jane Austen as my imaginary Best Friend Forever. Make Room for Ruth Bader Ginsburg, who would have gone to my high school for MUSIC, if her parents had let her · whose favorite artist is MATISSE. (I rest my case.)

Who went on to study the LAW because she wanted to combat the forces of INJUSTICE (McCarthyism) and graduated tied for FIRST in her CLASS at COLUMBIA Law School, but could not get HIRED as a LAWYER.

her secretaries would warn the clerks, according to one of them, that it was a turban day, "so that we wouldn't giggle when we saw her."

RBG's chambers are evidence of her finely attuned taste. There is a statue of Eleanor Roosevelt, conventional enough, but then RBG had the standard desk the Supreme Court justices have topped with a black granite. Although she has said her favorite artist is Matisse, given her pick of art from Washington museum collections (as all justices are), her choices were more obscure. She favors the mid-twentieth-century American artist Ben Cunningham, whose abstract work his biographer describes as combining "logic with imagination to add new dimensions to our experience of social confrontation and protest." Another favorite in the same geometrical, color-blocked vein is the German-born Josef Albers. (In 2011, she coyly said she wouldn't retire at least until she got her Albers back from a traveling exhibition. She estimated that would happen sometime in 2012. The day came and went.) She has borrowed paintings by Mark Rothko and Max Weber too.

A SPARROW,
EXCEPT IN HER DREAMS

RBG weeps at the opera. "She could get quite sentimental in movies," says Jane, but opera is in an emotional class of its own. RBG is often wistful about what could have been, had she only been born with the pipes. "If I had any talent that God could give me, I would be a great diva," she said.

"But sadly I have a monotone. And my grade school teachers were very cruel. They rated me a sparrow, not a robin." She sings anyway—but "only in the shower, and in my dreams."

It all started when eleven-year-old Kiki sat in a Brooklyn high school and watched, electrified, as a conductor named Dean Dixon conducted *La Gioconda*. She would also always remember that Dixon, an African American whose career thrived in Europe, was held back for reasons that had nothing to do with his talent. "In all the time he conducted in the U.S.," she told the *Santa Fe New Mexican* during one of her many visits to that city's summer opera festival, Dixon "was never called *maestro*," the customary respectful term for a conductor.

She and Marty were in the audience in 1961 when the legendary soprano Leontyne Price, an African American who battled racism on the stage and beyond, made her Metropolitan Opera debut in *Il Trovatore*. RBG remembered how a spotlight shone on the proud faces of Price's parents, a Mississippi mill worker and midwife. Decades later, RBG greeted Price at the court by taking her hand and exclaiming, "My, this magnificent woman." (When Price spontaneously sang at lunch, a reporter in the room was pretty sure Justice Kennedy, another opera fan, shed a tear.)

Opera ran in Marty's family too. Jane remembers that her paternal grandmother—RBG's beloved surrogate mother, Evelyn—listened every

Saturday to the Metropolitan Opera broadcasts, and Evelyn's own father had been a mechanic in an opera house in Odessa. When RBG and Marty were stationed in Oklahoma, they drove four hours to Dallas to hear the Metropolitan Opera's traveling performance and borrowed opera records from the library on base. Later, in New York, they shared a box at the Met and went every Friday, a secular Sabbath.

In Washington, they chose an apartment at the Watergate, right across the street from the John F. Kennedy Center, home to the Washington National Opera. Opera stars often speak of RBG's visits backstage, and her reverential but knowledgeable comments after the curtain falls. "We do consider her, informally, part of the family," the opera's president said. The justice also is a regular at the theater. "She has terrific taste and she's very knowledgeable," says Michael Kahn, artistic director of the Shakespeare Theatre Company, at whose wedding RBG officiated.

Being an opera fan on the highest court has its perks, including at least three onstage turns as an extra. One of these was with Scalia, in *Ariadne auf Naxos,* where RBG batted a fan and wore a white wig. One singer hopped on Scalia's lap. In a 2003 production of *Die Fledermaus,* she, Kennedy, and Breyer surprised everyone onstage when they were introduced as "three guests supreme from the Court Supreme." The best part? "Domingo was about two feet from me—it was like an electrical shock ran through me," RBG said.

RBG now oversees twice-annual opera and instrumental recitals at the court. As she put it in a speech, they "provide a most pleasant pause from the court's heavy occupations."

With Scalia onstage at the opera

10

BUT I JUST CAN'T QUIT

IRIN: *And when the time comes, what would you like to be remembered for?*

RBG: *Someone who used whatever talent she had to do her work to the very best of her ability. And to help repair tears in her society, to make things a little better through the use of whatever ability she has.*

—MSNBC interview, 2015

RBG DOES NOT LIKE to be told to slow down. In early 2009, just as people began counting her out, RBG was suddenly everywhere. Yes, she had been diagnosed with pancreatic cancer, but the tumor was small and detected early. Yes, a Democratic president had been elected with a Democratic Senate, laying the groundwork for a successor she could approve of. But RBG had a job to do, and she wasn't done yet.

There she was on February 23, smiling broadly from the bench less than three weeks after surgery, asking pointed questions at oral argument. There she was on February 24, taking her seat with the other justices at the first black president's inaugural speech to a joint session of Congress. "Some of us were angry with her, but we were wrong," David Schizer said. "We kept telling her to slow down, we kept telling her to take it easy." He sent her novels to read. "She wouldn't have any of it."

At Barack Obama's first speech to Congress in 2009

RBG, as ever, had a purpose. "First, I wanted people to see that the Supreme Court isn't all male," she said. Then, referring to Kentucky senator Jim Bunning, who had predicted she was at death's door, she added coolly, "I also wanted them to see I was alive and well, contrary to that senator who said I'd be dead within nine months." That night she paused to embrace the new president. "I've got a soft spot for Justice Ginsburg," Obama later said, and the feeling was mutual. "There was a rapport from the start between us," RBG said.

A decade earlier, her bout with a more advanced stage of colorectal cancer had given her a new outlook. "It is as though a special, zestful spice seasons my work and days," RBG said after her first recovery. "Each thing I do comes with a heightened appreciation that I am able to do it." That was doubly true the second time around. That spring, in a tribute to mark her fifteen terms on the bench, Chief Justice John Roberts offered his "warm congratulations on the occasion of your reaching the midpoint of your tenure," adding that she had "earned acclaim for your work ethic, intellectual rigor, precision with words and total disregard for the normal day-night work schedule adhered to by everyone else since the beginning of recorded history." If it really was the midpoint of her tenure, she'd be retiring only a year older than John Paul Stevens did, at age ninety-one.

None of these public displays of vigor stilled the retirement drumbeat. As Obama ran for reelection, Harvard Law School professor Randall Kennedy wrote what insiders had been whispering. Thurgood Marshall, for whom Kennedy had clerked, had retired in ill health, allowing George H. W. Bush to replace him with the ultraconservative Clarence Thomas. "Now, if Justice Ginsburg departs the Supreme Court with a Republican in the White House"—one that could be elected in 2012—"it is probable that the female Thurgood Marshall will be replaced by a female Clarence Thomas," Kennedy wrote. Technically, Kennedy aimed his advice at the five-years-younger Breyer too. "Those, like me, who admire their service might find it hard to hope that they will soon leave the Court—but service comes in many forms, including making way for others," he wrote. It was RBG, however, and not Breyer, who was essentially followed around with a microphone pointed at her, journalists asking her when she would just get out already.

After Barack Obama was reelected, the clamor didn't stop—after all, the Democrats faced an all but certain drubbing in the Senate in 2014, so there was a tiny window for Obama to appoint another liberal justice. (Democrats were indeed drubbed.) Women who had seen older women pushed out before or been pushed out themselves were furious at the pressure on RBG. Longtime Supreme Court chronicler Linda Greenhouse flat out called it sexist. "I am just pissed as hell at my friends, liberal law professors who urge her to retire," says Sylvia Law, a law professor who worked with RBG in the seventies, "because she is a complete unique and wonderful gem on the court. There are so many cases, especially technical cases, where you read the majority and it doesn't seem all that bad. And then you read Ruth's dissent, and you realize they have just done something terrible."

Justices try not to acknowledge what everyone else knows, which is that they tend to share many of the values of the president who appointed them. Each time she was asked about retirement, RBG walked a careful line. "There will be a president after this one, and I'm hopeful that that president will be a fine president," she said. In another interview, with Nina Totenberg, she went even further, offering, "Well, I'm very hopeful about 2016." One reporter said she nodded when it was said aloud that the next presidential election could bring the first female president. "Yes," RBG replied, "and wouldn't that be fantastic." A Hillary Clinton presidency might be the perfect moment for RBG to step down, but for now, she stays because she loves the job.

RBG has her own metric for when it's time to go. "When I forget the names of cases that I once could recite at the drop of a hat," she said, "I will know." She's not there yet.

SEEKING OUT THE
JOYS OF BEING ALIVE

"Do you want to see Marty's kitchen?" RBG recently asked her friend Anita Fial when she visited RBG's Watergate apartment. It is still Marty's kitchen, except these days, Jane comes down from New York and spends weekends at her mother's house cooking. In the freezer, Jane leaves behind little packages of meals, each marked "chicken" or "fish."

"Sometimes she'll be going to sleep just as I'm waking up," says Jane. "If I see that the paper has been brought inside, I know it's not because she got up early." Her mother still spends the weekends catching up on sleep she misses during the week.

Life after Marty has fallen into a kind of rhythm. In the old days, as she worked until the job was done, Marty would tell her that if she went to bed, in the morning everything would be clearer. "He was right," RBG said after Marty's death. "Sometimes I feel like I'm in a maze, then go to sleep thinking about the way out, and when I wake up in the morning, I see the path. But now there's no one telling me it's time to quit."

On mornings that the court is in session, the U.S. marshals make sure she's awake. "She lives off coffee," says her granddaughter Clara, who lived with her grandmother for a summer. Without it, "she will not engage."

Asked what had been the most surprising thing about growing older, RBG was characteristically crisp. "Nothing surprised me. But I've learned two things. One is to seek ever more the joys of being alive, because who knows how much longer I will be living? At my age, one must take things day by day." She added, "I had some trying times when my husband died. We'd been married for fifty-six years and knew each other for sixty. Now, four years later, I'm doing what I think he would have wanted me to do."

Her grandson, Paul, wishes Marty had been there to get a kick out of one recent scene. A couple of years ago, Paul, an actor, went to visit RBG in Washington. She'd given him his pick of plays that were supposed to be good. They were in the car, on their way back from somewhere, and as usual, there were two marshals—one driving, one in the passenger seat "looking stoic."

Paul says, "She asked the marshal if she could call the theater to book us tickets and warn them we'd be coming, because they always have to do their marshal security check. The lady marshal asked, 'What's the name of the show?'" RBG had chosen *Cock*, a play by Mike Bartlett. "It's called *Cock*," she told the marshal. "She could have been saying, 'The duke's red horse,'" says Paul. The marshal dutifully picked up the phone to secure tickets on behalf of Justice Ginsburg to *Cock*. Throughout it all, RBG sat, unperturbed, in the backseat. She had been going to the theater for a long time.

FREE TO BE . . . YOU AND ME

On April 28, 2015, thirty-seven-year-old Dan Canon had followed the rules. It was his first time taking a case to the Supreme Court, intimidating even if it weren't one of the most important civil rights cases of our time, *Obergefell v. Hodges*. The shaved-headed former musician turned civil rights lawyer was there to represent people whose marriages didn't count in Kentucky, because they were two men or two women. From the counsel's table, where Dan was sitting, he could have reached up and grabbed Justice Samuel Alito. He didn't.

Outside the court, there were preprinted posters about abomination, but also rainbow flags and a GRANDPARENTS FOR JUSTICE sign. There was one MARRY ME, SCALIA placard. For months, there had been calls for RBG to recuse herself, because she had performed two same-sex weddings shortly after the Supreme Court struck down the Defense of Marriage Act. She ignored them. Inside, as oral argument was in full swing, she offered a rebuttal to the argument that same-sex couples could not be let into marriage because the institution was rooted in millennia of tradition. "There was a change in the institution of marriage to make it egalitarian when it wasn't egalitarian," RBG cut in. "And same-sex unions wouldn't fit into what marriage was once." She herself had helped remake marriage, freeing it from the

laws circumscribing roles for men and women. A tradition that saw women as property would not have recognized RBG's own marriage.

Solicitor General Donald Verrilli, who was arguing on behalf of the government that day, wore the traditional morning coat with tails. There is a dress code at the Supreme Court for people like Canon too. "Appropriate attire for counsel is conservative business dress in traditional dark colors (e. g., navy blue or charcoal gray)," reads the official guide for lawyers bringing cases to the Supreme Court. Canon complied, wearing a navy suit jacket and a sky-blue button-down shirt. Before he had come to Washington, D.C., Canon had received a present from a law school friend and her wife, a schoolteacher. They had married in New York, but only one mother's name appeared on their son's birth certificate, because Kentucky voters decided Lori and Cristal's marriage shouldn't count. Under his button-down, Canon had a secret: He wore his friend's gift, a Notorious R.B.G. T-shirt.

Kennedy would be the one to write the opinion striking down bans on same-sex marriage. But it was RBG's image, rendered in rainbow and animation riding across the Supreme Court steps on a motorcycle, that dominated celebrations. RBG didn't author the majority opinions that term that, to the great shock of liberals, left intact or even expanded major portions of progressive legislation like the Affordable Care Act, the Fair Housing Act, and the Pregnancy Discrimination Act. But as the conservative justices turned on one another, RBG was credited with keeping the liberals together and finding a way to get to a fifth or even sixth vote. She put aside fiery dissents for the time being. After all, this time, her side had a shot at actually winning, and RBG wants to get things done, not just make some noise.

The comity on the court may be short lived, the product of conservative overreach rather than a leftward drift. Ten years into the Roberts court, much of what RBG has fought for remains at risk, starting with reproductive freedom. The court is poised to consider restrictions on abortion clinics that affect tens of millions of women. "We will never see a day when women of means are not able to get a safe abortion in this country," RBG told me. An abortion ban, she said, only "hurts women who lack the means to go someplace else." Public sector unions and affirmative action are already in the court's crosshairs.

RBG continues to use her voice on her own terms, and all around her are the signs of the progress that she and her allies have won. Visiting Columbia Law School in 2012, where she had once had to lead the fight for women as the only tenured female law professor, RBG paused for a moment. "I passed a door this morning that said 'Lactation room,'" she said. "How the world has changed." RBG, as much as anyone, has done that work.

Legacy is a topic RBG won't linger on, because it has a note of finality. But she will take stock. "In my life, what I find most satisfying is that I was a part of a movement that made life better, not just for women," RBG says. "I think gender discrimination is bad for everyone, it's bad for men, it's bad for children. Having the opportunity to be part of that change is tremendously satisfying. Think of how the Constitution begins. 'We the people of the United States in order to form a more perfect union.' But we're still striving for that more perfect union. And one of the perfections is for the 'we the people' to include an ever enlarged group." This expansion has been RBG's life's work. And it's not over yet.

APPENDIX

How to Be Like RBG

WORK FOR WHAT YOU BELIEVE IN

RBG saw injustice in the world and she used her abilities to help change it. Although the forces of "apathy, selfishness, or anxiety that one is already overextended" are "not easy to surmount," as she puts it, RBG urges us "to repair tears in [our] communities, nation, and world, and in the lives of the poor, the forgotten, the people held back because they are members of disadvantaged or distrusted minorities."

BUT PICK YOUR BATTLES

RBG survived the indignities of pre-feminist life mostly by deciding that anger was counterproductive. "This wonderful woman whose statue I have in my chambers, Eleanor Roosevelt, said, 'Anger, resentment, envy. These are emotions that just sap your energy," RBG says. "They're not productive and don't get you anyplace, so get over it.'" To be like RBG in dissent, save your public anger for when there's lots at stake and when you've tried everything else.

AND DON'T BURN YOUR BRIDGES

"Fight for the things that you care about," RBG advised young women, "but do it in a way that will lead others to join you." RBG always tells her clerks to paint the other side's arguments in the best light, avoiding personal insults. She is painstaking in presenting facts, on the theory that the truth is weapon enough.

DON'T BE AFRAID
TO TAKE CHARGE

RBG believes that "women belong in all places where decisions are being made." Back when many feminists were arguing that women spoke in a different voice, RBG observed the flaw in describing women as inherently different or even purer than men: "To stay uncorrupted, the argument goes, women must avoid internalizing 'establishment' values; they must not capitalize on opportunity presented by an illegitimate opportunity structure." RBG has used her establishment positions to fight for structural change and on behalf of the oppressed. More recently, she has also united the court's liberals under her leadership.

THINK ABOUT WHAT
YOU WANT, THEN DO THE WORK

When a young RBG suddenly was faced with the prospect of starting law school with a toddler, her father-in-law told her, "If you really want to study the law, you will find a way. You will do it." RBG says, "I've approached everything since then that way. Do I want this or not? And if I do, I'll do it."

BUT THEN ENJOY
WHAT MAKES YOU HAPPY

RBG gets out—a lot.

BRING ALONG YOUR CREW

"RBG was never in it to be the only one, to be the superstar that nobody could match," says fellow feminist attorney Marcia Greenberger. RBG mentored legions of feminist lawyers and happily welcomed Sotomayor and Kagan to the Supreme Court.

HAVE A SENSE OF HUMOR

A little goes a long way.

RBG's Favorite Marty Ginsburg Recipe

From *Chef Supreme*

PORK LOIN BRAISED IN MILK

INGREDIENTS

1 tbs. butter

2 tbs. vegetable oil (not olive oil)

2½ lbs. pork rib roast

Kosher salt and freshly ground pepper

2½ cups (or more) whole milk

PREPARATION

Have the butcher detach the meat in one piece from the ribs into 2 or 3 or more parts. You will use both meat and bones. Do not trim the fat from the meat.

You will need a heavy bottomed pot that can snuggly [*sic*] accommodate the pork and bones. Put in the butter and oil and turn heat to medium high. When the butter foam subsides, put in the meat, fat side down at first. As the meat browns, turn it so that the pork will brown evenly all around. Remove the meat to a plate, brown the bones, and return the meat to the pot.

Add salt, pepper, and 1 cup of milk. Add the milk slowly over low heat. There is a great risk the milk will boil over. After the milk has come to the simmer, for about 30 seconds, turn the heat down to barest minimum, and cover the pot with the lid slightly ajar. Cook at a low simmer for approximately one hour, turning the meat from time-to-time, until the milk has thickened (through evaporation) into nut-brown clusters. This may take a good deal more than one hour.

When the milk in the pot reaches that stage—not before—slowly and carefully add another cup of milk. Simmer for about 10 minutes and then cover the pot (lid on tight) and simmer on low heat 30 minutes.

After 30 minutes, set the lid slightly ajar and continue to cook at medium heat, turning the meat from time to time. When you see there is no more liquid milk in the pot, carefully add the final ½ cup of milk. Continue cooking on low heat, turning the meat from time to time, until the meat feels tender when prodded with a fork and all the milk has coagulated into small nut-brown clusters. In total, cooking will likely take nearly three hours. In the unlikely event the liquid in the pot has evaporated before the meat is fully cooked, add another ½ cup of milk and evaporate the liquid.

When the pork has become tender and all the milk in the pot has thickened into moderately dark clusters, remove and throw away the bones, transfer the meat to a cutting board, and after allowing it to set a bit, cut into slices between a ¼ inch and a ½ inch.

Meanwhile, tip the pot and spoon off most but not all the fat. There may be a lot of it. Be careful to leave behind all the coagulated brown clusters. Now add 3 tbs. water and boil the water away over high heat while using a wooden spoon to scrape cooking residue loose from the bottom and sides of the pot. Spoon all the pot juices over the pork and serve immediately.

NB: An alternative cut to pork loin is a 2 lb. piece of boneless pork butt, well tied. It's easier to cook because you have no bones to cook and, frankly, much juicier than loin, but it does not slice as neatly.

From
"R. B. Juicy"

By Kelly Cosby and Beth Gavin

[Introduction]

Yeah—this song is dedicated to all the judges that told me I'd never amount to nothin' because of my gender, to all the people that lived in their ivory towers that I was hustlin' in front of, that tried to buy me off by putting Susan B. Anthony on the dollar, and all the women in the struggle, you know what I'm sayin'?

[Verse]

It was all a dream
Back when I argued Reed v. Reed
Then once they put Sandy D up in the Dub D.C.
Janet Reno made the call
When Slick Willie chose me to sit; and now that I've been installed
I rock the black robe with my jabot
Sippin' tea while reading amici tales of woe
Way back, when I caught a lot of flak I held back
Now look where I'm at
Remember Frankfurter, duh-ha, duh-ha
He never thought a woman could go this far
Now I'm in the limelight cause I decide right
Court has moved right, but my dissents get cites
Born sinner, but definitely a winner
Defending women's rights cause unlike them, I'd been "her"
Peace to Willie, Jimmy C, and guess who?
Erwin Griswold, the ACLU
I'm blowing up the glass ceiling for good
Call the chamber, same number same hood
It's all good
Uh . . . and if you don't know, now you know, Nino

[Chorus]

You've been fighting for equal rights
From Kiki to RBG, you've reached those heights
You always fight, for equal justice
A diva in our eyes, originalists can't touch this

APPENDIX

From "Scalia/Ginsburg: A (Gentle) Parody of Operatic Proportions"

By Derrick Wang

SCALIA:

This court's so changeable—
As if it's never, ever known the law!
The Justices are blind!
How can they possibly spout this—?
The Constitution says absolutely nothing about this,
This right that they've enshrined—
When did the document sprout this?
The Framers wrote and signed Words that endured without this;
The Constitution says absolutely nothing about this!

. . .

GINSBURG:

How many times must I tell you,
Dear Mister Justice Scalia:
You'd spare us such pain
If you'd just entertain This idea . . .
(Then you might relax your rigid posture.)
You are searching in vain for a bright-line solution
To a problem that isn't so easy to solve—
But the beautiful thing about our Constitution
Is that, like our society, it can evolve.
For our Founders, of course, were great men with a vision,
But their culture restricted how far they could go,
So, to us, I believe, they bequeath the decision
To allow certain meanings to flourish—and grow.

Tributes to the Notorious RBG

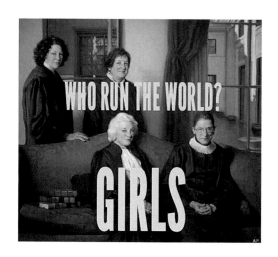

ALL THEM FIVES NEED TO LISTEN

WHEN A TEN IS TALKING

Woke up like this

flawless.

Supreme Court steps

flawless.

Alito stepping-

flawless.

writing a dissent

flawless.

Ruth Bader Ginsburg
Herstory in the making!

I'M NOT GON' GIVE UP

I'M NOT GON' STOP

I WILL WORK HARDER

I'M A SURVIVOR

Acknowledgments

THIS BOOK WAS BORN through the heroic efforts of Julia Cheif-fetz, our editor at Dey Street Books. We are indebted to her wisdom, perseverance, and patience. Also at Dey Street, we're grateful to the indefatigable Sean Newcott, Joseph Papa, Dale Rohrbaugh, Suet Chong, Tanya Leet, Lucy Albanese, Shannon Plunkett, Katy Riegel, Lynn Grady, Adam Johnson, Owen Corrigan, Michael Barrs, Nyamekye Waliyaya, and Zakiya Jamal.

Justice Ginsburg's family members—Jane Ginsburg, James Ginsburg, Clara Spera, and Paul Spera—graciously opened up their lives to us, for which we are thankful. We also appreciate Justice Ginsburg's friends, colleagues, and former clerks for their contributions. Our legal dream team, including Samuel Bagenstos, David S. Cohen, Janai Nelson, Margo Schlanger, Reva Siegel, and Neil Siegel, kept us on point. We cannot thank them enough. We were guided by the generous intellectual property advice of Ilana Broad, as well as by Jonathan A. Malki of Gottlieb, Rackman & Reisman, P.C.

Many staff members at the Supreme Court provided invaluable resources and support, including Kimberly McKenzie in Justice Ginsburg's chambers; Kathy Arberg, Patricia McCabe Estrada, Annie Stone, Tyler Lopez, and Sarah Woessner in the public information office; Steve Petteway, Daniel Sloan, Catherine Fitts, and Liza Liberman in the curator's office; and Clare Cushman of the Supreme Court Historical Society. We thank them all in particular for their ready assistance on our tight deadlines.

Many archivists and institutions helped us along the way, including Rebecca Beyer at Columbia Law School, Janet Donohue of Rutgers School of Law–Newark, Eisha Neely at Cornell University, Lesley Schoenfeld at Harvard Law School, Deborah Howlett at the ACLU of New Jersey, Lorraine Izzo at James Madison High School, and Lisa Miller at the Brearley School. We thank Lenora Lapidus and Erin White at the ACLU, Kathryn Mahaney and Judith S. Weis at Rutgers, and author John B. Railey, for additional research support. Thanks to William Blake and Hans Hacker, for sharing their research on oral dissents with us. At the Library of Congress manuscript division, Lewis Wyman and Jeffrey M. Flannery led the way. Brian Reynolds and Lacey Chemsak at Sony Music, along with the estate of Notorious B.I.G., came through for us. Micah Fitzerman-Blue and Frank William Miller Jr. made very important introductions.

Shout out to the community at #notoriousrbg on every platform, for being so goddamn amazing.

FROM IRIN

My agent, Linda Loewenthal of David Black Agency, has been my fierce advocate from the start. Anna Holmes and Rebecca Traister, my brilliant friends, mentors, and beloved feminist interlocutors, each in her own way made this book (and so much of my career) possible. Rachel Dry, always generous and insightful, was even more so in reading the manuscript.

At MSNBC, Beth Fouhy, Dafna Linzer, Richard Wolffe, Yvette Miley, and Phil Griffin have afforded me the privilege of reporting on women's rights on every platform, as well as the warm support to work on this book. Thanks also to Rachel Maddow, who championed my RBG interview, and to Sylvie Haller, who made it a reality. The folks at Yale Law School, in particular Priscilla Smith, Reva Siegel, and Jack Balkin, have welcomed me and taught me, as did Margot Kaminski. On both a personal and professional level, I

Yes, this is a selfie.

have learned so much from the astute chroniclers of the Supreme Court, including Linda Greenhouse, Jeffrey Toobin, Dahlia Lithwick, Lyle Denniston, Joan Biskupic, Pete Williams, and Art Lien. Sandra Bark and Elizabeth Green offered both friendship and hard-learned lessons from their experiences. I gratefully count Mollie Chen, Kristin Garcia, Steph Herold, Amelia Lester, Kaija-Leena Romero, Stella Safo, Adam Serwer, Aminatou Sow, Sarah Tucker, and Beth Wikler, among others, as both friends and teachers.

The Carmonsters—Ittai, Ella, Daria, Yahel, and Deni—are everything to me. I have been so blessed to have Haggai and Rakeffet Carmon as parents and unstinting supporters. RBG herself said it's important to have a "supportive man," but I was privileged to have much more than support. Thank you to Ari Richter, for seeing me through this with kindness, joy, and love.

FROM SHANA

I am grateful to my agent, Lindsay Edgecombe, as well as to Daniel Greenberg of Levine/Greenberg/Rostan Literary Agency, who guided me through a process that was entirely foreign at the outset and advocated on my behalf at every level. I am indebted to Ankur Mandhania for his notorious Facebook post, which sparked the fuse that became this phenomenon, as well as to my friend and colleague Frank Chi, whose words of advice and generous spare bedroom were essential on my many trips to Washington, D.C.

During my third year of law school, professor and vice dean Randy Hertz at NYU Law and Attorney Judith Harris at the Legal Aid Society's Bronx Juvenile Rights Practice were invaluable mentors and supporters of all of my endeavors both legal and otherwise, including this one, and were my biggest cheerleaders at all times.

At NYU, I appreciate Deirdre von Dornum, Norman Dorsen, Sylvia Law, Arthur Miller, Trevor Morrison, and Burt Neuborne, for their willingness to be a part of this project. I am also grateful to my fellow members of the Juvenile Defender Clinic, Law Review, Law Revue, CoLR, OUTLaw, Substantial Performance, and Defender Collective, for providing guidance, perspective, and welcome distraction at various stages.

I want to thank my longtime mentor and friend, Mia Eisner-Grynberg, who has been instrumental in helping me become the lawyer, and person, I am today, as well as my students and fellow coaches at Columbia Mock Trial, for always making my uptown treks worth the while.

To all of my friends in Philadelphia and New York: You've kept me sane through this process and I feel so lucky to have you as a constant in my life.

The support of my parents, Luda and Yuri Knizhnik, and of my brother, Ed Knizhnik, has been a driving force throughout my life—I quite literally could not have done this without them. Finally, thank you to Hillela Simpson for enduring my sleepless nights, for taking care of me in spite of myself, and for lovingly seeing me through this from start to finish.

In chambers

Notes

Chapter 1: Notorious

1 **That's her dissent collar** Fact-checking by Irin Carmon with Ruth Bader Ginsburg, in Boston, MA, May 29, 2015.

2 **without missing a day** *Id.*
about land and *Koontz v. St. Johns River Water Mgmt. Dist.*, 133 S. Ct. 2586 (2013).
custody case involving Indian law *Adoptive Couple v. Baby Girl*, 133 S. Ct. 2552 (2013).

3 **The case was Shelby County v. Holder** 133 S. Ct. 2612 (2013).
"But our country has changed" Opinion Announcement Part 1 at 7:25, *Shelby Cnty. v. Holder*, 133 S. Ct. 2612 (2013) (all opinion announcements available at oyez.org).
murdered civil rights activists See *Shelby Cnty. v. Holder*, 133 S. Ct. 2612, 2626 (2013).
High black voter turnout See *id.*
There were black mayors See *id.*
in an affirmative action case *Fisher v. Univ. of Tex.*, 133 S. Ct. 2411 (2013).
workplace discrimination cases *Vance v. Ball State Univ.*, 133 S. Ct. 2434 (2013); *Univ. of Tex. Sw. Med. Ctr. v. Nassar*, 133 S. Ct. 2517 (2013).

3 **"the court's disregard"** Opinion Announcement Part 2 at 4:19, *Univ. of Tex. Sw. Med. Ctr. v. Nassar*, 133 S. Ct. 2517 (2013).
Alito, who had written the majority opinion "Dana Milbank, Alito Is On a Roll: An Eye Roll," WASHINGTON POST, June 25, 2013.
Sandra Day O'Connor, sat in the section Mark Walsh, *A "View" from the Court: June 25, 2013*, SCOTUSBLOG (June 25, 2013).
"Justice Ginsburg has filed" Opinion Announcement Part 1 at 8:15, *Shelby Cnty. v. Holder*, 133 S. Ct. 2612 (2013).

4 **"Hubris is a fit word"** *Shelby Cnty. v. Holder*, 133 S. Ct. 2612, 2648 (2013) (Ginsburg, J., dissenting).
"throwing away your umbrella" *Id.* at 2650.
"what was once the subject" Opinion Announcement Part 2 at 1:22, *Shelby Cnty. v. Holder*, 133 S. Ct. 2612 (2013).

5 **getting angry was a waste** *E.g.*, Jeffrey Rosen, *The New Look of Liberalism on the Court*, NEW YORK TIMES, Oct. 5, 1997 [hereinafter Rosen, *The New Look of Liberalism*].
sometimes it helped to be a little deaf *E.g.*,

Association of American Law Schools, *Engendering Equality: A Conversation with Justice Ginsburg*, YouTube.com (Feb. 20, 2015) [hereinafter AALS, *Engendering Equality*].

5 ***broke a half-century-long record*** Richard Wolf, *Ginsburg's Dedication Undimmed After 20 Years on Court*, USA Today, Aug. 1, 2013.

"if there is a steadfast commitment" Opinion Announcement Part 2 at 9:59, *Shelby Cnty. v. Holder*, 133 S. Ct. 2612 (2013).

6 ***"Can't spell truth without Ruth."*** Interview by Shana Knizhnik with Aminatou Sow; interview by Irin Carmon with Frank Chi.

7 ***"schoolmarmish"*** Alan Dershowitz, *And the Winner Is . . .*, Washington Times, June 16, 1993; David Von Drehle, *Conventional Roles: Hid a Revolutionary Intellect*, Washington Post, Jul. 18, 1993 [hereinafter Von Drehle, *Conventional Roles*].

the wrong kind of feminist See Jeffrey Rosen, *The Book of Ruth*, New Republic, Aug. 2, 1993.

"a dinosaur" Margaret Carlson, *The Law According to Ruth*, Time, June 24, 2001.

insufficiently radical Interview by Shana Knizhnik with Burt Neuborne.

a dull writer Transcript of *NOW with Bill Moyers* (PBS television broadcast, May 3, 2002).

by comedian Amy Schumer Jennifer Konerman, *Amy Schumer's Marketing Ploy for Season 3*, Brief: a promaxbda publication (Mar. 31, 2015).

the show Scandal *It's Good to Be Kink*, Scandal (ABC television broadcast, Mar. 19, 2015).

on The Good Wife *The Deconstruction*, The Good Wife (CBS television broadcast, Apr. 26, 2015).

recurring Saturday Night Live character *Dakota Johnson/Alabama Shakes*, Saturday Night Live (NBC television broadcast, Feb. 28, 2015); *Scarlett Johansson/Wiz Khalifa*, Saturday Night Live (NBC television broadcast, May 2, 2015).

8 ***"no-nonsense people are rewarded"*** Interview by Shana Knizhnik with Aminatou Sow.

"It's hard for me to think of someone" Interview by Irin Carmon with David Schizer.

9 ***"I would not have thought of her as hip"*** Interview by Irin Carmon with James Ginsburg.

"a crucial expansion of the American imagination" Rebecca Traister, *How Ruth Bader Ginsburg Became the Most Popular Woman on the Internet*, New Republic, Jul. 10, 2014.

"Women lose power with age" Interview by Irin Carmon with Gloria Steinem.

"her willingness to be a public figure" Interview by Shana Knizhnik with Burt Neuborne.

"But what really changed" Jeffrey Rosen, *Ruth Bader Ginsburg Is an American Hero*, New Republic, Sept. 28, 2014.

11 ***"She's not just deliberative"*** Rosen, *The New Look of Liberalism*.

"Ruth is almost pure work" Pam Lambert, *Determined Judge*, Cornell Alumni News, November 1980, at 67.

two of her old ACLU colleagues Von Drehle, *Conventional Roles*.

12 ***"a flaming radical"*** Interview by Shana Knizhnik with Cynthia Fuchs Epstein.

"She subordinated her own persona" Interview by Shana Knizhnik with Burt Neuborne.

"It would not include me" Conversation with Justice Ruth Bader Ginsburg and Theodore "Ted" B. Olson, C-SPAN (Dec. 17, 2013).

13 ***RBG felt a little faint*** E.g., Jess Bravin, *Justice Ginsburg Undergoes Heart Procedure to Treat Coronary Blockage*, Wall Street Journal, Nov. 27, 2014.

"I would be glad to greet the clever creators" Letter from Ruth Bader Ginsburg to Shana Knizhnik, Aminatou Sow, and Frank Chi (Oct. 8, 2014) (on file with author).

Chapter 2: Been in This Game for Years

15 ***justices bunk together*** Ruth Bader Ginsburg, *The Supreme Court: A Place for Women*, Vital Speeches of the Day, May 1, 2001, at 420–24.

"Was invited to sit in the Chief Justice's seat" Letter from Sarah Grimké to Sarah Wattles (Dec.

23, 1853) (Weld-Grimké Papers, William L.
Clements Library, University of Michigan).

15 *Myra Bradwell* Bradwell v. Illinois, 83 U.S. 130
(1873).
"The method of communication" Brief for the
Petitioner, *Struck v. Sec'y of Def.,* 409 U.S. 1071
(1972) (No. 72-178), 1972 WL 135840, at 39.
Mills v. United States 164 U.S. 644 (1897).

16 *"When you say you have 'no available graduates'"*
David L. Weiden and Artemus Ward, *Sorcerers'
Apprentices: 100 Years of Law Clerks at the United
States Supreme Court* 88 (2006).

17 **Brown v. Board of Education of Topeka** 347 U.S.
483 (1954).
"The study of law was unusual" Sandra Pullman,
*Tribute: The Legacy of Ruth Bader Ginsburg and
WRP Staff,* ACLU (Feb. 19, 2006).
"it was only fair to pay me modestly" Ruth Bader
Ginsburg, *Remarks on Women's Progress in the Legal
Profession in the United States,* 33 TULSA LAW
REVIEW 13, 15 (1997).

18 *"tricky question of Swedish civil procedure"* Adam
Liptak, *Kagan Says Path to Supreme Court Was
Made Smoother Because of Ginsburg's,* NEW YORK
TIMES, Feb. 10, 2014.

19 *"The Department of Justice, I am sure"* Oral
Argument at 75:51, *Phillips v. Martin-Marietta
Corp.,* 400 U.S. 542 (1971).
Reed v. Reed Brief for Appellant, *Reed v. Reed,*
404 U.S. 71 (1971) (No. 70-4), 1971 WL 133596.
Roe v. Wade 410 U.S. 113 (1973).
Doe v. Bolton 410 U.S. 179 (1973).
"This right of privacy" Roe, 410 U.S. at 153.
first-ever casebook Kenneth M. Davidson,
Ruth Bader Ginsburg, and Herma Hill Kay,
Sex-Based Discrimination: Text, Cases and Materials
(1974).

20 **Bush v. Gore** 531 U.S. 98 (2000).
"The wisdom of the court's decision" David G.
Savage, *Ginsburg Rebukes Justices for Intervening in
Fla. Vote,* LOS ANGELES TIMES, Feb. 3, 2001.

21 *"the lone woman"* Darragh Johnson, *Sandra Day
O'Connor, Well Judged Women's Group Honors

Pioneering High Court Justice, WASHINGTON POST,
Mar. 7, 2006.

21 **Gonzales v. Carhart** 550 U.S. 124 (2007).
"pretends that its decision protects women" Opinion
Announcement at 7:27, *Gonzales v. Carhart,* 550
U.S. 124 (2007).
Lilly Ledbetter Ledbetter v. Goodyear Tire and
Rubber Co., 550 U.S. 618 (2007).
"I hear that Justice Ginsburg has been working"
Jeffrey Toobin, *The Oath: The Obama White House
and the Supreme Court* 118 (2012).
"I wanted people to see" Joan Biskupic, *Ginsburg
Back with Grit, Grace,* USA TODAY, Mar. 6, 2009.
"I like the idea that we're all over the bench"
Joan Biskupic, *Justice Ginsburg Reflects on Term,
Leadership Role,* USA TODAY, June 30, 2011.

22 *"skim milk marriage"* Oral Argument at 70:51,
United States v. Windsor, 133 S. Ct. 2675 (2013).
"the blessings and the strife" Robert Barnes,
Ginsburg to Officiate Same-Sex Wedding,
WASHINGTON POST, Aug. 30, 2013.
Burwell v. Hobby Lobby 134 S. Ct. 2751 (2014).
not "100 percent sober" Ariane de Vogue, *Ginsburg
and Scalia on Parasailing, Elephants and Not Being
"100% Sober,"* CNN (Feb. 13, 2015).

23 *"The court, I fear, has ventured"* 134 S. Ct. 2805
(Ginsburg, J., dissenting).

Chapter 3: I Got a Story to Tell

25 *"I feel like a very lucky girl"* Bruce Weber, *Latest
Chapter in a Photographer's Worldwide Project,* NEW
YORK TIMES, Sept. 19, 1996.
"my son the doctor, the lawyer" Von Drehle,
Conventional Roles.
"She ran with a group of girls" Interview by Irin
Carmon with Hesh Kaplan.
Camp Che-Na-Wah David Von Drehle, *Redefining
Fair with a Simple Careful Assault: Step-by-Step
Strategy Produced Strides for Equal Protection,*
WASHINGTON POST, Jul. 19, 1993 [hereinafter Von
Drehle, *Redefining Fair*].

26 *"This was a girl who was an adventurer"* Ruth

Bader Ginsburg Interview, ACAD. OF ACHIEVEMENT: A MUSEUM OF LIVING HISTORY (Aug. 17, 2010) [hereinafter ACAD. OF ACHIEVEMENT].

26   *"I learned to love the smell"* AALS, *Engendering Equality.*

Judy Coplon Interview by Irin Carmon with Hesh Kaplan.

the smell of death Von Drehle, *Conventional Roles.*

Kiki's friends gathered Fact-checking by Irin Carmon with Ruth Bader Ginsburg, in Boston, MA (May 29, 2015).

27   *Celia Amster* Fred Strebeigh, *Equal: Women Reshape American Law* 11 (2009).

On the day before the ceremony Id.

28   *the minyan* Abigail Pogrebin, *Stars of David: Prominent Jews Talk About Being Jewish* 19–20 (2007).

"That meant always conduct yourself" Larry Josephson, *A Conversation with Justice Ruth Bader Ginsburg: Her Life as a Woman, a Jew and a Judge,* ONLY IN AMERICA (Sept. 2, 2004) [hereinafter ONLY IN AMERICA].

Celia had quietly scraped together Strebeigh, *Equal,* at 12; Von Drehle, *Conventional Roles;* ONLY IN AMERICA.

"It was one of the most trying times" Supreme Court Justices Kennedy, Ginsburg, Scalia, and O'Connor, C-SPAN (Oct. 8, 2009) [hereinafter C-SPAN, *Supreme Court Justices*].

mental map of every women's bathroom AALS, *Engendering Equality.*

29   *"The women were a heck of a lot smarter"* Scott Rosenthal, *Students in D.C. Meet Justice Ginsburg '54,* CORNELL DAILY SUN, Apr. 16, 2007.

"You could drop a bomb" Interview by Shana Knizhnik with Anita Fial.

10 P.M. curfew Von Drehle, *Conventional Roles.*

boys were allowed ACAD. OF ACHIEVEMENT.

30   *Kiki tried, and then dropped* ONLY IN AMERICA.

Vladimir Nabokov Ruth Bader Ginsburg: From Brooklyn to the Bench, CORNELL UNIVERSITY (Sept. 22, 2014) [hereinafter CORNELL, *From Brooklyn to the Bench*].

30   *professor Robert E. Cushman* Id.

"a war against racism" Id.

Marcus Singer Cornell Relieves Marcus Singer of Teaching Duties, HARVARD CRIMSON, Nov. 24, 1954; Von Drehle, *Conventional Roles.*

"I got the idea that being a lawyer" Justice Ruth Bader Ginsburg Remarks at Georgetown University Law Center, C-SPAN (Feb. 4, 2015) [hereinafter Georgetown Remarks].

the first boy she ever met CORNELL, *From Brooklyn to the Bench.*

31   *Marty's gray Chevy* Beth Saulnier, *Justice Prevails: A Conversation with Ruth Bader Ginsburg '54,* CORNELL ALUMNI MAGAZINE, Nov./Dec. 2013 [hereinafter Saulnier, *Justice Prevails*].

"There was a long, cold week" Georgetown Remarks.

"I have no doubt that in our case" Jay Mathews, *The Spouse of Ruth: Marty Ginsburg, the Pre-Feminism Feminist,* WASHINGTON POST, June 19, 1993 [hereinafter Mathews, *The Spouse of Ruth*].

"Ruth was a wonderful student" Claudia MacLachlan, *Mr. Ginsburg's Campaign for Nominee,* NATIONAL LAW JOURNAL, June 27, 1993, at 33.

His father, Morris Interview by Irin Carmon with Jane Ginsburg.

failed her driving test five times Fact-checking by Irin Carmon with Ruth Bader Ginsburg, in Boston, MA (May 29, 2015).

"to be in the same discipline" Mathews, *The Spouse of Ruth.*

Marty had dropped AALS, *Engendering Equality.*

"Ruth always intended" Mathews, *The Spouse of Ruth.*

32   *married in the Ginsburgs' living room* Ruth Bader Ginsburg, *The Honorable Ruth Bader Ginsburg: Associate Justice of the Supreme Court of the United States,* in THE RIGHT WORDS AT THE RIGHT TIME 116 (Marlo Thomas, ed. 2004) [hereinafter THE RIGHT WORDS AT THE RIGHT TIME].

eighteen people present Id.

"I'm going to tell you the secret" AALS, *Engendering Equality.*

"My mother-in-law meant" THE RIGHT WORDS AT THE RIGHT TIME.

32   *Fort Sill base* AALS, *Engendering Equality.*
civil service exam Von Drehle, *Conventional Roles*; fact-checking by Irin Carmon with Ruth Bader Ginsburg, in Boston, MA (May 29, 2015).

33   *"Ruth, if you don't want to go to law school"* Saulnier, *Justice Prevails.*

34   *"to combine the power and beauty"* Tamar Lewin, *Herbert Wechsler, Legal Giant, Is Dead at 90,* NEW YORK TIMES, Apr. 28, 2000.
"I wanted to know more" E.g., Judith Richards Hope, *Pinstripes and Pearls: The Women of the Harvard Law Class of '64 Who Forged an Old Girl Network and Paved the Way for Future Generations* 105 (2003).
"We try to take people" Lynn Gilbert, *Particular Passions: Ruth Bader Ginsburg* (1988).
"something strange and singular" Ruth Bader Ginsburg, Keynote Speech at Harvard Law School Celebration 25 (Apr. 15, 1978) (on file with the Library of Congress Manuscript Division).

35   *"You felt in class"* ACAD. OF ACHIEVEMENT.
Lamont Library Nomination of Ruth Bader Ginsburg to Be an Associate Justice of the Supreme Court of the United States: Hearings Before the S. Comm. on the Judiciary, 103rd Cong. 134 (1993) [hereinafter *Senate Judiciary Hearings*].

36   *Rhoda Isselbacher* Jill Abramson, *Class of Distinction: Women Find Success After Harvard Law '59, Despite the Difficulties—Judge Ginsburg's Classmates Balanced Lives, Careers, Helped Shape Profession—"Ecstatic" Over Appointment,* WALL STREET JOURNAL, Jul. 20, 1993, at A1 [hereinafter Abramson, *Class of Distinction*].
Cancer, which had already ONLY IN AMERICA

37   *she could get by* Robert Barnes, *The Question Facing Ruth Bader Ginsburg: Stay or Go?,* WASHINGTON POST, Oct. 4, 2013 [hereinafter Barnes, *The Question Facing Ruth Bader Ginsburg*].
"Only your first and second years" ONLY IN AMERICA.
Griswold refused Georgetown Remarks.
Hazel Gerber Interview by Irin Carmon with David Schizer.

37   *"the smartest person on the East Coast"* David Margolick, *Trial by Adversity Shapes Jurist's Outlook,* NEW YORK TIMES, June 25, 1993.

38   *Marty wrote a letter* Martin D. Ginsburg, *Spousal Transfers: In '58, It Was Different,* HARVARD LAW REVIEW, May 6, 1977, at 11.
"Just think what else" Ruth Bader Ginsburg, *The Changing Complexion of Harvard Law School,* 27 HARVARD WOMEN'S LAW JOURNAL 303, 305 (2004).
Felix Frankfurter Neil A. Lewis, *Rejected as a Clerk, Chosen as a Justice,* NEW YORK TIMES, June 15, 1993.
Paul Bender Todd C. Peppers and Artemus Ward, *In Chambers: Stories of Supreme Court Law Clerks and Their Justices* (2012).

39   *Judge Learned Hand* Strebeigh, *Equal,* at 37.
They hired Pauli Murray ONLY IN AMERICA.
Gerald Gunther AALS, *Engendering Equality.*
it didn't work out Id.

40   *"'Young lady, I'm not looking at you'"* Saulnier, *Justice Prevails.*
"Ruth, how would you like" *Georgetown Remarks*; *Professor Hans Smit Remembered as an "Odysseus" at Memorial Service,* COLUMBIA LAW SCHOOL (Feb. 20, 2012).
Anders Bruzelius Daniel Friedland, *Scandinavian Trip This Summer,* THE TRANSCRIPT, Apr. 11, 1966, at 6.
"Both men and women have one main role" Linda Haas, *Equal Parenthood and Social Policy: A Study of Parental Leave in Sweden* 55 (1992).

41   *Actress Sherri Finkbine Symposium Honoring the 40th Anniversary of Justice Ruth Bader Ginsburg Joining the Columbia Law Faculty: A Conversation with Justice Ginsburg,* COLUMBIA LAW SCHOOL (Feb. 10, 2012) [hereinafter *Columbia Symposium*].
Ingmar Bergman movies sans subtitles Fact-checking by Irin Carmon with Ruth Bader Ginsburg, in Boston, MA (May 29, 2015).
the best English-language book Adam Liptak, *Kagan Says Path to Supreme Court Was Made Smoother Because of Ginsburg's,* NEW YORK TIMES, Feb. 10, 2014.

Chapter 4: Stereotypes of a Lady Misunderstood

43   *"I say the constitutional principle"* ACAD. OF ACHIEVEMENT.

RBG had skipped lunch E.g., Jay Boyar, *Supreme Sightseeing*, ORLANDO SENTINEL, Nov. 13, 2005.

Wearing her mother's pin Elinor Porter Swiger, *Women Lawyers at Work* 56 (1978).

"Mr. Chief Justice, and may it please the court" Oral Argument at 17:19, *Frontiero v. Richardson*, 411 U.S. 677 (1973) [hereinafter Frontiero Oral Argument].

Sharron Frontiero *Frontiero v. Richardson*, 411 U.S. 677 (1973).

44   **Reed v. Reed** 404 U.S. 71 (1971).

"the same stereotype" Frontiero Oral Argument, at 17:32.

"Mrs. Ruth Ginsburg" Seth Stern and Stephen Wermiel, *Justice Brennan: Liberal Champion* 394 (2010).

45   *"They help keep woman in her place"* Frontiero Oral Argument, at 25:22.

Behind her sat Brenda Feigen Interview by Irin Carmon with Brenda Feigen.

"Sex, like race, is" Frontiero Oral Argument, at 20:52.

46   *"'I ask no favor for my sex'"* Frontiero Oral Argument, at 27:33.

"Very precise female" Fred Strebeigh, *Equal: Women Reshape American Law* 55 (2009) [hereinafter Strebeigh, *Equal*].

Simone de Beauvoir's The Second Sex Von Drehle, *Conventional Roles*.

Rutgers School of Law was looking *Georgetown Remarks.*

"Robes for Two Ladies" Sue Weinstock, *Robes for Two Ladies*, NEWARK STAR-LEDGER, June 4, 1970.

47   *"you have a husband who earns"* Pam Lambert, *Ginsburg and Rabb: Setting Precedents*, COLUMBIA, Summer 1980, at 10.

"Is there another?" Fact-checking by Irin Carmon with Ruth Bader Ginsburg, in Boston, MA (May 29, 2015).

48   **She ran to her mother-in-law's closet** Ruth Bader Ginsburg, Remarks at Hawaii Women Lawyers' Tea (Oct. 30, 1986) (on file with the Library of Congress Manuscript Division) [hereinafter Hawaii Remarks].

"Each day, just before class" Ruth Bader Ginsburg, Remarks for Rutgers School of Law–Newark (Apr. 11, 1995) (on file with the Library of Congress Manuscript Division) [hereinafter Rutgers Remarks].

"Yes, dear" Strebeigh, *Equal*, at 113.

New Jersey branch Rutgers Remarks.

49   **asked her to teach** Id.

"Land, like woman, was meant to be possessed" Von Drehle, *Conventional Roles*.

federal class-action pay-discrimination claim Ruth Bader Ginsburg, *Remarks on Women's Progress in the Legal Profession in the United States*, 33 TULSA LAW REVIEW 13, 15 (1997).

50   *"The female carrier hats"* Letter from Laney Kaplan to American Civil Liberties Union (Aug. 20, 1971) (on file with the Library of Congress Manuscript Division).

"The insistence on sexual identification" Letter from Ruth Bader Ginsburg to William H. Blount, Postmaster General (Sept. 17, 1971) (on file with the Library of Congress Manuscript Division).

51   **Charles E. Moritz** E.g., *Conversation with Justice Ruth Bader Ginsburg and Goodwin Liu*, C-SPAN AND AMERICAN CONSTITUTION SOCIETY FOR LAW AND POLICY (June 13, 2015).

"some down and dirty women's rights" Strebeigh, *Equal*, at 25.

52   *"pluck her from obscurity"* Id.

"when biological differences" Brief for Petitioner-Appellant, *Moritz v. Commissioner of Internal Revenue*, 469 F.2d 466 (10th Cir. 1972) (No. 71-1127) (on file with the Library of Congress Manuscript Division).

"woman co-counsel in that case???" Letter from Ruth Bader Ginsburg to Mel Wulf (Apr. 6, 1971) (on file with the Library of Congress Manuscript Division).

52 *"Maybe she plucked herself"* Strebeigh, *Equal*, at 27.

53 *Gwendolyn Hoyt* Hoyt v. Florida, 368 U.S. 57 (1961).
"still regarded as the center" Id. at 62.
"give rise to moral and social problems" Goesaert v. Cleary, 335 U.S. 464, 466 (1948).
RBG had met a lawyer A Conversation with Justice Ruth Bader Ginsburg: Her Life as a Woman, a Jew and a Judge, ONLY IN AMERICA (Sept. 2, 2004).

54 *"Jane Crow and the Law"* Linda K. Kerber, *No Constitutional Right to Be Ladies* 202 (1998).
challenged the all-white and all-male jury White v. Crook, 251 F. Supp. 401 (Ala. 1966).
Murray's work was all over Brief for Appellant, *Reed v. Reed,* 404 U.S. 71 (1971) (No. 70-4), 1971 WL 133596.

55 *"standing on their shoulders"* Georgetown Remarks.
"It's just not done" Interview by Shana Knizhnik with Burt Neuborne.
the world was finally ready to listen Georgetown Remarks.

56 *RBG's Brief in* Reed v. Reed Brief for Appellant, *Reed v. Reed,* 404 U.S. 71 (1971) (No. 70-4), 1971 WL 133596, at 5–21.

58 *"High Court Outlaws Sex Discrimination"* High Court Outlaws Sex Discrimination, NEW YORK POST, Nov. 22, 1971.
the Playboy Bunny Von Drehle, *Redefining Fair.*

59 *a computer-generated list* E.g., Ruth Bader Ginsburg, *Advocating the Elimination of Gender-Based Discrimination: The 1970s New Look at the Equality Principle at University of Cape Town, South Africa* (Feb. 10, 2006).
"The distance to equal opportunity" Ruth Bader Ginsburg, *Prospectus for the Women's Rights Project of the American Civil Liberties Union* (1972) (on file with the Library of Congress Manuscript Division).
Frontiero v. Richardson 411 U.S. 677, 684 (1973).
"Traditionally, such discrimination" Id. at 684.

60 *"My wife became resigned long ago"* Marlene Cimons, *Family Ruling on Rehnquist*, LOS ANGELES TIMES, Dec. 14, 1973, at F7.

60 *"Real change, enduring change"* Senate Judiciary Hearings, at 122.
"We usually followed her advice" Rosen, *The New Look of Liberalism.*

61 *"Ginsburg lacks the dash"* Mitchel Ostrer, *Columbia's Gem of the Motion: A Profile of Ruth Bader Ginsburg,* JURIS DOCTOR, Oct. 1977, at 35 [hereinafter Ostrer, *Columbia's Gem of the Motion*].
course evaluation COLUMBIA LAW SCHOOL COURSE EVALUATIONS, CONFLICT OF LAWS (on file with the Library of Congress Manuscript Division).
"scored a major coup" Lesley Oelsner, *Columbia Law Snares a Prize in the Quest for Women Professors,* NEW YORK TIMES, Jan. 26, 1972, at 36 [hereinafter Oelsner, *Columbia Law Snares a Prize*].
"Did the Times *rule out Ms.?"* Letter from Ruth Bader Ginsburg to Lesley Oelsner (Jan. 26, 1972) (on file with the Library of Congress Manuscript Division).
"The only confining thing" Oelsner, *Columbia Law Snares a Prize.*
the women at Columbia Ruth Bader Ginsburg, Remarks at Columbia Law School, May 1980 (on file with the Library of Congress Manuscript Division).

62 *"getting visible the support"* Letter from Women's Affirmative Action Coalition to Ruth Bader Ginsburg (Feb. 16, 1972) (on file with the Library of Congress Manuscript Division).
"grave and costly mistake" Letter from Ruth Bader Ginsburg to William J. McGill, President of Columbia University (Aug. 22, 1972) (on file with the Library of Congress Manuscript Division).
"tended too much to begin screaming" Letter from Walter Gellhorn to American Civil Liberties Union and New York Civil Liberties Union (Aug. 28, 1972) (on file with the Library of Congress Manuscript Division).

62 *"There was a certain hostility"* Interview by Shana Knizhnik with Diane Zimmerman.

63 *"the days of 'negative action'"* Ruth Bader Ginsburg, *Introduction*, 1 COLUMBIA JOURNAL GENDER AND LAW 1 (1991).

"Women Working" Brenda Feigen, *Not One of the Boys: Living Life as a Feminist* (2000).

64 *Captain Susan Struck* Struck v. Sec'y of Def., 460 F.2d 1372 (9th Cir. 1971), *vacated as moot*, 409 U.S. 1071 (1972); Ian Shapiro, *Still Speaking in a Judicial Voice: Ruth Bader Ginsburg Two Decades Later*, 122 YALE LAW JOURNAL ONLINE 257 (2013).

67 *RBG wasn't ready to let go* Ruth Bader Ginsburg, *Speaking in a Judicial Voice*, 67 NEW YORK UNIVERSITY LAW REVIEW 1185 (1992).

"broad enough to encompass" Roe v. Wade, 410 U.S. 113, 153 (1973).

"It's not about the woman alone" Emily Bazelon, *The Place of Women on the Court*, NEW YORK TIMES, Jul. 7, 2009 [hereinafter Bazelon, *The Place of Women on the Court*].

upheld a ban on federal funding Harris v. McRae, 448 U.S. 297 (1980).

68 *"grounded on stereotypes"* Brief for the American Civil Liberties Union and Equal Rights Advocates, Inc. as Amicus Curiae, *General Electric Co. v. Gilbert*, 519 F.2d 661 (4th Cir. 1975) (No. 74-1557) (on file with the Library of Congress Manuscript Division).

"The notion is that when the woman" Ostrer, *Columbia's Gem of the Motion*.

69 *"As for that, it takes two"* Letter from Ruth Bader Ginsburg to Mary Just Skinner, Re: *Crawford v. Cushman* (Feb. 13, 1973) (on file with the Library of Congress Manuscript Division).

Geduldig v. Aiello 417 U.S. 484 (1974).

female employees sued General Electric Gen. Elec. Co. v. Gilbert, 429 U.S. 125 (1976).

"an in-and-out noon-hour treatment" Strebeigh, *Equal*, at 121.

69 *"voluntarily undertaken"* Gen. Elec. Co. v. Gilbert, 429 U.S. 125, 136 (1976).

GE hadn't left out any Id. at 151 (Brennan, J., dissenting).

"She was very much a leader" Interview by Shana Knizhnik with Judith Lichtman.

Pregnancy Discrimination Act 42 U.S.C. § 2000(e) et seq.

70 **Stephen *"played homemaker"*** Stephen Wiesenfeld, *Letter to the Editor*, NEW BRUNSWICK HOME NEWS, Nov. 27, 1972.

"the familiar stereotype that" Brief for Appellee, *Wiesenfeld v. Wiesenfeld*, 420 U.S. 636 (1975) (No. 73-1892), 1974 WL 186057.

"Just as the female insured individual's" Id.

71 *"My first reaction was"* Mildred Hamilton, *Ruth Wins One for ERA*, NEW JERSEY EXAMINER, Mar. 24, 1975, at 21.

"Given the purpose of enabling" Weinberger v. Wiesenfeld, 420 U.S. 636, 651 (1975).

"Wiesenfeld *is part of an evolution*" Ruth Bader Ginsburg, *The Supreme Court Back on Track:* Weinberger v. Wiesenfeld (on file with the Library of Congress Manuscript Division).

choices men like Stephen Wiesenfeld made Cary C. Franklin, *The Anti-Stereotyping Principle in Constitutional Sex Discrimination Law*, 85 NEW YORK UNIVERSITY LAW REVIEW 83 (2010).

72 *"It is not women's liberation"* Margolick, *Trial by Adversity*.

"Men need to learn" Ruth Bader Ginsburg, Keynote Speech at Harvard Law School Celebration 25 (Apr. 15, 1978) (on file with the Library of Congress Manuscript Division) [hereinafter Harvard Law School Celebration 25 Keynote].

"The time may come" Letter from Erwin N. Griswold to Ruth Bader Ginsburg (Oct. 17, 1978) (on file with the Library of Congress Manuscript Division).

73 *"without denying to white men"* Letter from Ruth

Bader Ginsburg to Erwin N. Griswold (Oct. 19, 1978) (on file with the Library of Congress Manuscript Division).

73 *"what better place"* Harvard Law School Celebration 25 Keynote.
"before very long, the old boys" Id.

Chapter 5: Don't Let 'Em Hold You Down, Reach for the Stars

77 *"it just wasn't in the realm"* ACAD. OF ACHIEVEMENT.
Like a bride Makers Profile: Ruth Bader Ginsburg: U.S. Supreme Court Justice, MAKERS (Feb. 26, 2013).
he'd chosen her for being ACAD. OF ACHIEVEMENT.
"moral imagination has cooled" The Supreme Court, Transcript of President's Announcements and Judge Ginsburg's Remarks, NEW YORK TIMES, June 15, 1993.
"Ruth Bader Ginsburg cannot be called a liberal" Id.

78 *"I wasn't important at all"* Claudia MacLachlan, Mr. Ginsburg's Campaign for Nominee, NATIONAL LAW JOURNAL, June 27, 1993, at 33.
"There were probably scores" Id.

79 *Marty was a tax lawyer* Jan Crawford Greenburg, Supreme Conflict: The Inside Story of the Struggle for Control of the United States Supreme Court (2007).
Marty did make them lunch Id.
"push her out on the cultural left" George Stephanopoulos, All Too Human: A Political Education 292 (2008).
"we'll have a little ceremony" ACAD. OF ACHIEVEMENT.
"The White House handlers had no time" Id.
"the civil rights movement of the 1960s" Id.
"it contributes to the end of the days" Id.

80 *"Celia Amster Bader, the bravest and strongest* Id.
"I wonder how many gender-discrimination" Nina Totenberg, Notes on a Life, in THE LEGACY OF RUTH BADER GINSBURG 3 (Scott Dodson, ed. 2015).

81 *The new group's president* Phone interview by Shana Knizhnik with Lynn Hecht Schafran.

81 *Notes from 2d Circuit Interview* Handwritten notes, Ruth Bader Ginsburg, Notes from 2nd Circuit Interview (on file with the Library of Congress Manuscript Division).
"I am heartened by the people" Letter from Ruth Bader Ginsburg to Diane Serafin Blank (Mar. 19, 1979) (on file with the Library of Congress Manuscript Division).

82 *"all increases in numbers"* Letter from Barbara Allen Babcock to the Attorney General (Mar. 12, 1979) (on file with the Library of Congress Manuscript Division).
"militant feminist interpretations" 126 CONGRESSIONAL RECORD E39 (daily ed. Jan. 22, 1980) (statement of Rep. John M. Ashbrook).
"gross distortion of my views" Letter from Ruth Bader Ginsburg to Professor Herbert Wechsler (Jan. 28, 1980) (on file with the Library of Congress Manuscript Division).
"Republican Judiciary Committee members" Nina Totenberg, Ginsburg: Will "She" Sail as Smoothly as "He" Would?, LEGAL TIMES OF WASHINGTON, May 26, 1980.
senator Strom Thurmond voted Senate Judiciary Hearings, at 664.
confirmed unanimous 126 CONGRESSIONAL RECORD 15238 (daily ed. June 18, 1980).
sat on the floor giggling Interview by Shana Knizhnik with Diane Zimmerman.

83 *"genuinely open-minded"* Gerald Gunther, Ruth Bader Ginsburg: A Personal, Very Fond Tribute, 20 UNIVERSITY OF HAWAI'I LAW REVIEW 583, 586 (1998).
"heedful of limitations" Id.
"the most independent, thoughtful" Id.
"What do you mean, 'wives'?" Abramson, Class of Distinction.
a hand was usually outstretched Conversation with Justice Ginsburg and Joan C. Williams at UC Hastings, C-SPAN (Sept. 15, 2011) [hereinafter UC Hastings Conversation].

84 *"She was widely regarded"* Susan H. Williams and David C. Williams, Sense and Sensibility: Justice

Ruth Bader Ginsburg's Mentoring Style as a Blend of Rigor and Compassion, 20 UNIVERSITY OF HAWAI'I LAW REVIEW 589, 590 (1998).

84 *"I don't see myself in the role"* On Becoming a Judge: Socialization to the Judicial Role, 69 JUDICATURE 139, 145 (1985).
in a speech she gave Ruth Bader Ginsburg, *Speaking in a Judicial Voice*, 67 NEW YORK UNIVERSITY LAW REVIEW 1185 (1992).

85 *"halted a political process" Id.* at 1208.
"They felt that **Roe** *was so precarious"* Interview by Shana Knizhnik with Burt Neuborne.
"The women are against her" Daniel Patrick Moynihan and Steven R. Weisman, *Daniel Patrick Moynihan: A Portrait in Letters of an American Visionary* 605–6 (2012).
Erwin Griswold's speech Stephen Labaton, *Senators See Easy Approval for Nominee,* NEW YORK TIMES, June 16, 1993.

86 *A* **Legal Times** *study in 1988* Clarence Page, *President Clinton's "Stealth" Justice,* CHICAGO TRIBUNE, June 20, 1993 [hereinafter Page, *President Clinton's "Stealth" Justice*].
"Robert Bork's America" 133 CONG. REC. S9188 (daily ed. Jul. 1, 1987) (statement of Sen. Edward Kennedy).
"harbors no animosity" Ruth Bader Ginsburg: "So Principled, She's Unpredictable," BUSINESSWEEK, June 27, 1993.
"Is Ruth Bader Ginsburg another Thurgood Marshall Page, *President Clinton's "Stealth" Justice.*
a "sweet lady" Id.
lawyers found her a "picky" Alan Dershowitz, *And the Winner Is . . . ,* WASHINGTON TIMES, June 16, 1993, at G1.
"a 'difficult person'" Id.
"denigrating the memory of a hero" Id.
"The president could not have made" Stephen Wermiel, *Justice Brennan: Liberal Champion* (2010).

87 *"Committee Republicans are looking"* Robert Barnes, *Clinton Library Release of Papers on Ginsburg, Breyer Nominations Offer Insight, Some*
Fun, WASHINGTON POST, June 8, 2014.

87 *"I will not do anything to disparage" UC Hastings Conversation.*
My Grandma Is Very Special *Senate Judiciary Hearings,* at 46.

88 **Strom Thurmond did press RBG** *Id.* at 146.
"a judge must do" Id.
"You are good, judge" Id.
"Anyone who knew her knows" Interview by Irin Carmon with Alisa B. Klein.
"avowed devotion to privilege for females" Senate Judiciary Hearings, at 506 (statement of Nellie J. Gray, President of March for Life Education and Defense Fund).
"When government controls that decision" Id. at 207.

89 *"no secretary, no law clerk"* C-SPAN, *Supreme Court Justices.*
"One justice or another will say" Id.

90 *Virginia Military Institute's* United States v. Virginia, 518 U.S. 515 (1996).
"designed as a place to teach" Oral Argument at 8:15, *United States v. Virginia,* 518 U.S. 515 (1996).
"men have got to become accustomed" Id. at 23:56.

91 *From RBG's Opinion in* United States v. Virginia, 518 U.S. 515, 532–57 (1996).

93 *the court had snuck in* United States v. Virginia, 518 U.S. 515, 567–68 (1996) (Scalia, J., dissenting).
"VMI case as the culmination of the 1970s" Ruth Bader Ginsburg, *Advocating the Elimination of Gender-Based Discrimination: The 1970s New Look at the Equality Principle at University of Cape Town, South Africa* (Feb. 10, 2006).
"Dear Bill, See how the light you shed" Stephen Wermiel, *Justice Brennan: Liberal Champion,* at 408.
"It was a good day" Interview by Irin Carmon with David Toscano.
RBG got a letter Ruth Bader Ginsburg, *A Conversation with Associate Justice Ruth Bader Ginsburg,* 84 UNIVERSITY COLUMBIA LAW REVIEW 909, 929 (2013).

Chapter 6: Real Love

95 *"It's not sacrifice; it's family."* Stephen Labaton, *The Man Behind the High Court Nominee,* New York Times, June 17, 1993.

Proof on Broadway *Women's Law and Public Policy Fellowship Annual Conference on Women and the Law,* C-SPAN (Sept. 25, 2003) [hereinafter *Women's Law and Public Policy Remarks*].

jokingly chasing Marty around her desk Interview by Irin Carmon with David Toscano.

96 *"stood very low in his class"* Joan Biskupic, *Martin Ginsburg, Justice's Husband, Dies,* USA Today, June 28, 2010.

"The model was of equality" Interview by Irin Carmon with Margo Schlanger.

97 *"He thought that I must be pretty good"* Jessica Weisberg, *Supreme Court Justice Ruth Bader Ginsburg: I'm Not Going Anywhere,* Elle, Sept. 23, 2014.

"I think that the most important thing" Nina Totenberg, *Notes on a Life,* in The Legacy of Ruth Bader Ginsburg 6 (Scott Dodson, ed. 2015).

"life's partner" Senate Judiciary Hearings, at 46.

"among the pioneers" Id. at 561 (statement of Stephen Wiesenfeld).

"devoted to protecting the deservedly rich" Jeffrey Toobin, *Heavyweight,* New Yorker, Mar. 11, 2013 [hereinafter Toobin, *Heavyweight*].

98 *"Fortunately, in my marriage"* Elizabeth Vrato, *The Counselors: Conversations with 18 Courageous Women Who Have Changed the World* 176 (2002).

"It was impossible to praise him" Interview by Shana Knizhnik with Burt Neuborne.

"I have been supportive" Labaton, *The Man Behind the High Court Nominee.*

"In the course of a marriage" Irin Carmon, *Ruth Bader Ginsburg on Marriage, Sexism, and Pushups,* MSNBC (Feb. 17, 2015).

99 *RBG crashed her car into a gate* Bill Hewitt, *Feeling Supreme,* People, June 27, 1993.

"Yes, but you don't go!" Maria Simon, *Reflections,* 20 University of Hawai'i Law Review 599, 600 (1998).

99 *his advice was for her to go to sleep* Balancing Public and Private Life, C-SPAN (May 17, 1997).

"he always made me feel" Id.

"to learn about each other" Totenberg, *Notes on a Life.*

"I had a job that, quite literally, required" Women's Law and Public Policy Remarks.

100 *tuna casserole* Jay Mathews, *The Spouse of Ruth: Marty Ginsburg, the Pre-Feminism Feminist,* Washington Post, June 19, 1993.

Escoffier cookbook Id.; fact-checking by Irin Carmon with Ruth Bader Ginsburg, in Boston, MA (May 29, 2015).

"I had seven things I could make" UC Hastings Conversation.

"Mommy should be phased out" Carmon, *Ruth Bader Ginsburg on Marriage.*

"Mommy does the thinking" James Ginsburg, *Thoughts on Marty,* in Chef Supreme: Martin Ginsburg 91 (Clare Cushman, ed. 2011).

he got used to people Interview by Irin Carmon with James Ginsburg.

101 *Ginsburgs' shelves held* Jessica Gresko, *New Cookbook: Eating Like a Supreme Court Justice,* Boston.com (Dec. 20, 2011).

"I hate Marty Ginsburg" Rosen, *The New Look of Liberalism.*

good thing Bill Clinton hadn't asked Barnes, *The Question Facing Ruth Bader Ginsburg.*

"What is very hard for most women" Acad. of Achievement.

Marty threw himself into caring Von Drehle, *Conventional Roles.*

"Jane's mommy works" Interview by Irin Carmon with Jane Ginsburg.

102 *"one of the biggest sweatshops"* Symposium Honoring the 40th Anniversary of Justice Ruth Bader Ginsburg Joining the Columbia Law Faculty: A Conversation with Justice Ginsburg, Columbia Law School (Feb. 10, 2012).

"Your son is now four years old" Von Drehle, *Conventional Roles.*

"But it was also the way things were" Balancing Public and Private Life.

102 *"This child has two parents"* Ruth Bader Ginsburg, *Remarks for George Mason University School of Law Graduation May 22, 1993*, 2 George Mason Independent Law Review 1, 2–5 (1993).
"How far could he go?" Interview by Irin Carmon with James Ginsburg.
Women Lawyers at Work Elinor Porter Swiger, *Women Lawyers at Work* 59–61 (1978).

103 *"I'd know she was very disappointed"* Rosen, *The New Look of Liberalism*.
writing an essay every day Interview by Irin Carmon with James Ginsburg.
Jane would write down each time Interview by Irin Carmon with Jane Ginsburg.

104 *It never occurred to them* UC Hastings Conversation.
Ladies Dining Room Ruth Bader Ginsburg, *Foreword*, in Malvina Shanklin Harlan, Some Memories of a Long Life, 1854–1911, at xvi (2003).
Dennis Thatcher Society Balancing Public and Private Life.

105 *"Marty liked being a spouse"* Cathleen Douglas Stone, *Lunch with Marty*, in Chef Supreme, at 75.
"It's your birthday" Interview by Shana Knizhnik with Trevor Morrison.
"there was something disarming" Interview by Irin Carmon with Kate Andrias.
"Marty got up and walked" Todd C. Peppers and Artemus Ward, *In Chambers: Stories of Supreme Court Law Clerks and Their Justices* (2012).
"Marty was always my best friend" Full Interview with Supreme Court Justice Ruth Bader Ginsburg, MSNBC (Feb. 17, 2015) [hereinafter *MSNBC Interview*].
"If my first memories are of Daddy cooking" Ginsburg, *Thoughts on Marty*, at 125.

107 *Christian group at a public university* Christian Legal Society v. Martinez, 561 U.S. 661 (2010).
"My father would certainly not have wanted" Interview by Irin Carmon with Jane Ginsburg.
As Chief Justice Roberts read Jeffrey Toobin, *Without a Paddle: Can Stephen Breyer Save the Obama Agenda in the Supreme Court*, New Yorker, Sept. 27, 2010.

107 *the folded American flag* Mark Sherman, *Ginsburg Anticipates Being 1 of 3 Female Justices*, Seattle Times, Aug. 4, 2010.

Chapter 7: My Team Supreme

109 *"She's Justice Ginsburg. I'm Justice O'Connor"* Rosen, *The New Look of Liberalism*.
"a way of saying we are all in this together" C-SPAN, *Supreme Court Justices*.

110 *"She'll hold her own"* Bazelon, *The Place of Women on the Court*.
"a fabulous judge" Adam Liptak, *From Justice Thomas, a Little Talk About Race, Faith, and the Court*, New York Times, Sept. 17, 2012.
Race, Gender, and Power in America Rosen, *The New Look of Liberalism*.
"I have always enjoyed Nino" Joan Biskupic, *Ginsburg, Scalia Strike a Balance*, USA Today, Dec. 25, 2007.
"If you can't disagree ardently" Barnes, *The Question Facing Ruth Bader Ginsburg*.
"I think the current Chief is very good" Toobin, *Heavyweight*.
"gave me a little jab" MSNBC Interview.

111 *"It was his natural reaction"* Adam Liptak, *Court Is "One of the Most Activist," Ginsburg Says, Vowing to Stay*, New York Times, Aug. 24, 2013.
"Every 5–4 decision" Toobin, *Heavyweight*.
Kennedy has appeared onstage Roxanne Roberts, *Opera's Supreme Moment*, Washington Post, Sept. 8, 2003.
he infuriated RBG with his patronizing Linda Greenhouse, *Justices Back Ban on Abortion Method*, New York Times, Apr. 19, 2007.
"She didn't even interview me" Adam Liptak, *Kagan Says Path to Supreme Court Was Made Smoother Because of Ginsburg's*, New York Times, Feb. 10, 2014.

112 *"a sign women were there to stay"* Conversation

with Justice Ruth Bader Ginsburg and Theodore "Ted" B. Olson, C-SPAN (Dec. 17, 2013) [hereinafter *Conversation with Ted Olson*].

112 *"I'm Sandra" and "I'm Ruth" T-shirts* Ruth Bader Ginsburg, *A Woman's Voice May Do Some Good*, Politico (Sept. 25, 2013).
"She's Justice Ginsburg. I'm Justice O'Connor" Rosen, *The New Look of Liberalism*.

113 *"'It's OK, Ruth'"* Bazelon, *The Place of Women on the Court.*
"big sister" Dennis Abrams, *Sandra Day O'Connor: U.S. Supreme Court Justice* 100 (2009).
"This is your first opinion for the Court" Ginsburg, *A Woman's Voice.*
"wearing my bra and my wedding ring" Joan Biskupic, *Sandra Day O'Connor* (2009).
O'Connor's votes diverged more from RBG's Jeffrey Rosen, *The Woman's Seat*, New York Times Magazine, Oct. 16, 2005.
They proved women had diverse views Feels Isolated on Court, Washington Post, Jan. 28, 2007.
Planned Parenthood v. Casey 505 U.S. 833 (1992).
RBG and O'Connor hosted dinners Ginsburg on Same-Sex Marriage, Women's Rights, Health, Bloomberg (Feb. 12, 2015).
gave her advice Biskupic, *Sandra Day O'Connor.*

114 *"Everyone rallied around me"* UC Hastings Conversation.
Nevada Department of Human Resources v. Hibbs 538 U.S. 721, 736 (2003).
"Most people had no idea" Bazelon, *The Place of Women on the Court.*

115 *"I was fascinated by him"* Joan Biskupic, *American Original: The Life and Constitution of Supreme Court Justice Antonin Scalia* 89 (2010).
"Scalia came in and liberals edged" Margaret Carlson, *The Law According to Ruth*, Time, June 24, 2001.
the two share a love of opera C-SPAN, *Supreme Court Justices*; Biskupic, *Ginsburg, Scalia Strike a Balance.*
"Scalia kills it and Marty cooks it" Biskupic, *Ginsburg, Scalia Strike a Balance.*

115 *"I never heard them talk"* Phone interview by Shana Knizhnik with Paul Spera.
"It was quite a magnificent" UC Hastings Conversation.

116 *"I love him"* Biskupic, *American Original*, at 277.
Alito has sometimes joined Charlie Campbell, *Shakespeare in Court: Justices Hold Mock Trial Based on Bard's Tragedy*, Time (May 15, 2013).
There was no proof Alito Dale Russakoff, *Alito Disavows Controversial Group*, Washington Post, Jan. 12, 2006.

117 *"Yes. Less than I once did"* MSNBC Interview.
"try to teach through my opinions" Id.
"I would hope that a wise Latina woman" Charlie Savage, *A Judge's View of Judging Is on the Record*, New York Times, May 14, 2009.
"I thought it was ridiculous" Bazelon, *The Place of Women on the Court.*

118 *"Ginsburg relented and followed"* Joan Biskupic, *Breaking In: The Rise of Sonia Sotomayor and the Politics of Justice* (2014).
young Kagan had demanded her rabbi The Justice Ruth Bader Ginsburg Distinguished Lecture on Women and the Law, C-SPAN (Feb. 3, 2014) (introductory remarks by Justice Ginsburg).

119 *"More than any other person"* Id. (Kagan's speech about RBG).
no "shrinking violets" Conversation with Ted Olson.
"When there are nine" Georgetown Remarks.
"underestimating the justice" Tom Goldstein, Oral Argument as a Bridge Between the Briefs and the Court's Opinion, in The Legacy of Ruth Bader Ginsburg 221 (Scott Dodson, ed. 2015).
"not often, but sometimes, a justice" C-SPAN, *Supreme Court Justices.*

120 *"Dear Ruth, I might join your opinion"* Id.
"I try to be fair" Jeffrey Rosen, *Ruth Bader Ginsburg Is an American Hero*, New Republic, Sept. 28, 2014.
"heady experience" Ruth Bader Ginsburg, *Lecture: The Role of Dissenting Opinions*, 95 Minnesota Law Review 1 (2010).
RBG joked that he ruined her weekend Barnes, *The Question Facing Ruth Bader Ginsburg.*

120 *"I thought to myself, 'Don't stay up all night'"* MSNBC Interview.
"Richard, what are you doing there?" Phone interview by Shana Knizhnik with Richard Primus.

121 *"After that, the Supreme Court police"* Phone interview by Irin Carmon with Samuel Bagenstos.
"Kennedy is a morning person" Phone interview by Shana Knizhnik with Daniel Rubens.
"If my opinion runs more than twenty pages" Interview with Bryan Garner, LawProse (2006).
"Get it right and keep it tight" Maria Simon, *Reflections*, 20 University of Hawai'i Law Review 599, 599 (1998).
"If you can say it in plain English" Interview with Bryan Garner.
"I think that law" Id.
She had crossed out and rewritten Phone interview by Irin Carmon with David Shizer.

122 *"Marty wanted me to go to a movie"* Interview by Irin Carmon with David Schizer.
"My writing style tends to be" Symposium Honoring the 40th Anniversary of Justice Ruth Bader Ginsburg Joining the Columbia Law Faculty: A Conversation with Justice Ginsburg, Columbia Law School (Feb. 10, 2012).
"She had an acute sense" Interview by Irin Carmon with Alisa Klein.
"We all laugh about how fast she is" Barnes, *The Question Facing Ruth Bader Ginsburg.*
"her tolerance for conversation silence" Phone interview by Shana Knizhnik with Richard Primus.

123 *"Five Mississippi Rule"* Id.
"You would slowly start backing up" Phone interview by Shana Knizhnik with Paul Berman.
"I wasn't the first guy in the world" Phone interview by Irin Carmon with David Post.
"When fathers take equal responsibility" Rosen, *The New Look of Liberalism.*

124 *"I was so pleased to see"* Linda Greenhouse, *Word for Word: A Talk with Ginsburg on Life and the Court*, New York Times, Jan. 7, 1994.
"Of course, a lot of women have to do it" Phone interview by Irin Carmon with David Post.

124 *"Justice Ginsburg was so delighted"* Susan H. Williams and David C. Williams, *Sense and Sensibility: Justice Ruth Bader Ginsburg's Mentoring Style as a Blend of Rigor and Compassion*, 20 University of Hawai'i Law Review 589 (1998).
"So that is one very important thing" Todd C. Peppers, *In Chambers: Stories of Law Clerks and Their Justices* (2012).

125 *"I didn't know you had a special friend"* Phone interview by Shana Knizhnik with Paul Berman.
"she said, 'by the power vested in me'" Id.
"The week that the Ginsburg clerk teams" Phone interview by Irin Carmon with Scott Hershovitz.
"We expect more, even from the junior justice" Id.

Chapter 8: Your Words Just Hypnotize Me

127 *"Anyway, hope springs eternal"* Columbia Symposium.
"I think when it's wrong" Nina Totenberg, *Justice Scalia, the Great Dissenter, Opens Up*, NPR (Apr. 28, 2008).
Dred Scott *Dred Scott v. Sandford*, 60 U.S. (19 How.) 393 (1857).
Plessy v. Ferguson 163 U.S. 537 (1896).

128 **Bush v. Gore** 531 U.S. 98 (2000).
"It was described as a circus" Op-Ed, *My Florida Recount Memory*, New York Times, Nov. 20, 2010.
"value one person's vote" Bush v. Gore, 531 U.S. at 104–5.
"Federal courts defer to state high courts'" Bush v. Gore, 531 U.S. at 143 (Ginsburg, J., dissenting).
"The footnote sent Scalia into a rage" Jeffrey Toobin, *Too Close to Call: The Thirty-Six-Day Battle to Decide the 2000 Election* 266–67 (2002).
"December storm over the U.S. Supreme Court" Ginsburg Recalls Florida Recount Case, New York Times, Feb. 4, 2001.

129 *"all of us really do prize"* Transcript of *NOW with Bill Moyers* (PBS television broadcast May 3, 2002).
"my chief" Ruth Bader Ginsburg, *Constitutional Adjudication in the United States as a Means of*

Advancing the Equal Stature of Men and Women Under the Law, 26 Hofstra Law Review 263, 267–70 (1997) ("my now Chief"); *A Conversation Between Justice Ruth Bader Ginsburg and Professor Robert A. Stein,* 99 Minnesota Law Review 1, 11 (2014) ("later became my chief").

129 *"So, where are they?"* Scott Conroy, *Madame Justice,* CBS (Oct. 1, 2006).

130 *"You would have to ask the political leaders"* Id. **Why not ask a justice who had hired no women?** Linda Greenhouse, *Women Suddenly Scarce Among Justices' Clerks,* New York Times, Aug. 30, 2006.

131 *"one-at-a-time curiosity"* Joan Biskupic, *Ginsburg "Lonely" Without O'Connor; The Remaining Female Justice Fears Message Sent by Court Composition,* USA Today, Jan. 25, 2007.
"The word I would use to describe" Id.
Planned Parenthood v. Casey 505 U.S. 833 (1992).
"The ability of women to participate" Id., 856.
"More and more I think that science" Stephanie B. Goldberg, *The Second Woman Justice,* ABA Journal, Oct. 1993, at 42.

132 *"undue burden"* Casey, 505 U.S. at 874 (1992). ("Only where state regulation imposes an undue burden on a woman's ability to make this decision does the power of the State reach into the heart of the liberty protected by the Due Process Clause.")
Bill Clinton, surrounded by women Bill Clinton on Vetoing the Partial Birth Abortion Ban, PBS NewsHour (Apr. 10, 1996).
the movement went to sympathetic states E.g., *Stenberg v. Carhart,* 530 U.S. 914 (2000).
"Whatever this particular ban does" Opinion announcement at 24:46, *Stenberg v. Carhart,* 530 U.S. 914 (2000).
"The State may promote but not endanger" Stenberg, 530 U.S. at 931.
RBG wrote separately Stenberg, 530 U.S. at 951–52 (Ginsburg, J., concurring).
Kennedy, who found Stenberg, 530 U.S. at 957–59 (Kennedy, J., dissenting).

132 *Bush triumphantly signed a new federal* The Partial-Birth Abortion Ban Act of 2003, Public Law 108–5, 117 Stat. 1201.

133 *Only one lower court judge* Planned Parenthood v. Casey, 947 F.2d 682, 719 (3d Cir. 1991) aff'd in part, rev'd in part, 505 U.S. 833 (1992).
Gonzales v. Carhart 550 U.S. 124, 159 (2007).
"While we find no reliable data" Id. at 159–60.
"if all women were as sensitive as he is" Dahlia Lithwick, *Father Knows Best,* Slate (Apr. 18, 2007).
Kennedy's opinion insulted" Bazelon, *The Place of Women on the Court.*
"our obligation is to define" Gonzales v. Carhart, 550 U.S. 124, 182 (2007) (Ginsburg, J., dissenting) (quoting *Planned Parenthood v. Casey,* 505 U.S. 833, 850 [1992]).
the court was "differently composed" Opinion Announcement at 15:35, *Gonzales v. Carhart* 550 U.S. 124 (2007).

134 *Excerpt from RBG's Dissent* Gonzales v. Carhart, 550 U.S. 124, 171–91 (2007) (Ginsburg, J., dissenting).

136 *Lilly Ledbetter* Lilly Ledbetter, *Grace and Grit: My Fight for Equal Pay and Fairness at Goodyear and Beyond* (2013).
too long to sue Ledbetter v. Goodyear Tire and Rubber Co., 421 F.3d 1169, 1182–83 (11th Cir. 2005).
"We were around the same age" Ledbetter, *Grace and Grit.*
"within 180 days after" Ledbetter v. Goodyear Tire and Rubber Co., 550 U.S. 618, 619 (2007).
"It's the story of almost every working woman" Toobin, *Heavyweight.*

137 **Ledbetter v. Goodyear Tire** Opinion Announcement at 4:00–10:57, *Ledbetter v. Goodyear Tire and Rubber Co.,* 550 U.S. 618 (2014).

140 *campaign-finance limits* Federal Election Commission v. Wisconsin Right to Life, Inc., 551 U.S. 449 (2007).
"The way to stop discrimination" Parents involved in *Cmty. Sch. v. Seattle Sch. Dist. No. 1,* 551 U.S. 701, 748 (2007).

140 **"She has always been regarded"** Linda Greenhouse, *Oral Dissents Give Ginsburg a New Voice,* New York Times, May 31, 2007.

"I will continue to give voice to my dissent" *The Nation in Brief: No Turning the Clock Back on Abortion, Justice Ginsburg Says,* Washington Post (Oct. 22, 2007).

Obama signed the Lilly Ledbetter Fair Pay Act Sheryl Gay Stolberg, *Obama Signs Equal-Pay Legislation,* New York Times, Jan. 29, 2009.

141 **thirteen-year-old Arizona student Savana Redding** *Safford Unified Sch. Dist. v. Redding,* 557 U.S. 364 (2009).

"I'm trying to work out why is this a major thing" Oral Argument at 43:40, *Safford Unified Sch. Dist. v. Redding,* 557 U.S. 364 (2009).

"It wasn't just that they were stripped to their underwear" Oral Argument at 44:12, *Safford Unified Sch. Dist. v. Redding,* 557 U.S. 364 (2009).

"never been a thirteen-year-old girl" Joan Biskupic, *Ginsburg: Court Needs Another Woman,* USA Today (Oct. 5, 2009).

142 **"It can happen even in the conferences** *Id.*

the school's strip-searching of Redding *Redding,* 557 U.S. at 368 (2009).

"As we live, we can learn" *MSNBC Interview.*

"they provide a basis" Richard L. Hasen, *Roberts' Iffy Support for Voting Rights,* Los Angeles Times (Aug. 3, 2005).

"I think it is attributable" Oral Argument at 51:48, *Shelby Cnty. v. Holder,* 133 S. Ct. 2612 (2013).

143 **"I think the current court will go down in history"** Richard Wolf, *Ginsburg's Dedication Undimmed After 20 Years on Court,* USA Today (Aug. 1, 2013).

"But the storm is raging" Lani Guinier, *Justice Ginsburg: Demosprudence Through Dissent,* in The Legacy of Ruth Bader Ginsburg 214 (Scott Dodson, ed. 2015).

144 **Shelby County v. Holder** *Shelby Cnty. v. Holder,* 133 S. Ct. 2612, 2633–51 (2013) (Ginsburg, J., dissenting).

148 **"Such an untested prophecy"** *Bush v. Gore,* 531 U.S. 98, 144 (2000) (Ginsburg, J., dissenting).

149 **"The stain of generations"** *Gratz v. Bollinger,* 539 U.S. 244, 304 (2003) (Ginsburg, J., dissenting).

Chapter 9: I Just Love Your Flashy Ways

151 **"we do ten at a time"** *MSNBC Interview.*

Bryant Johnson has been her trainer Interview by Irin Carmon with Bryant Johnson.

153 **"I told Ruth she should sit in the back"** Interview by Shana Knizhnik with Burt Neuborne.

"President Clinton was looking for a young jurist" Claudia MacLachlan, *Mr. Ginsburg's Campaign for Nominee,* National Law Journal, June 27, 1993, at 33.

A little practice, the players agreed Maria Simon, *Reflections,* 20 University of Hawai'i Law Review 599, 600 (1998).

She surprised everyone by picking Interview by Shana Knizhnik with Burt Neuborne.

"the whole works" *MSNBC Interview.*

155 **"How many push-ups can you do?"** Interview by Irin Carmon with Jeffrey Toobin.

160 **"You know, the standard robe"** Robert Barnes, *Justices Have Differing Views of Order in the Court,* Washington Post, Sept. 4, 2009.

"It looks fitting for dissent" *Exclusive: Ruth Bader Ginsburg on Hobby Lobby, Roe v. Wade, Retirement and Notorious R.B.G.,* Yahoo News Video (Jul. 31, 2014).

161 **"It was glorious"** *Id.*

"I think you just have to do" *Supreme Court Justice Elena Kagan Interview,* C-SPAN (Dec. 9, 2010).

"'we are all in the business of impartial judging'" Brian Lamb and Susan Swain, *The Supreme Court: A C-SPAN Book, Featuring the Justices in Their Own Words* 116 (2013)

162 **"I didn't know anyone who made robes"** Adam Liptak, *The Newest Justice Takes Her Seat,* New York Times, Sept. 8, 2009.

"The judiciary is not a profession" *Stars and Storm Volunteers Mingle at Glamour Women of the Year Awards,* CBS News (Nov. 13, 2012).

"When she turned up at the Senate" Carrie

Donovan, *Style: Security Blankets,* NEW YORK TIMES, Oct. 31, 1993.

162 *"It was hard not to be struck"* Rosen, *The New Look of Liberalism.*

A secretary at Marty's law firm Women's Law and Public Policy Remarks.

163 *Marty wasn't much of a shopper* Interview by Irin Carmon with David Schizer.

"Ginsburg chose to wear" Jeffrey Toobin, *The Nine: Inside the Secret World of the Supreme Court* 143 (2007).

"She kept calling it 'that thing on your face'" Interview by Shana Knizhnik with Clara Spera.

165 *"logic with imagination"* Cindy Nemser, *Ben Cunningham: A Life with Color* (1989).

she wouldn't retire Toobin, *Heavyweight.*

166 *RBG weeps at the opera* Barnes, *The Question Facing Ruth Bader Ginsburg.*

"She could get quite sentimental" Interview by Irin Carmon with Jane Ginsburg.

"If I had any talent that God could give" Justice Ruth Bader Ginsburg Remarks at Georgetown University Law Center, C-SPAN (Feb. 4, 2015).

"In all the time he conducted" Anne Constable, *Santa Fe a Favorite Summer Getaway for Justice Ginsburg,* SANTA FE NEW MEXICAN, Aug. 23, 2014.

"My, this magnificent woman" Anthony Tommasini, *Justices Greet Diva: It's Ardor in the Court,* NEW YORK TIMES, Oct. 31, 2008, at C8.

Opera ran in Marty's family too Interview by Irin Carmon with Jane Ginsburg.

167 *"We do consider her, informally, part of the family"* Marisa M. Kashino, *Stage Presence: Ruth Bader Ginsburg's Love of the Arts,* WASHINGTONIAN (Oct. 10, 2012).

"terrific taste" Interview by Irin Carmon with Michael Kahn.

at least three onstage turns Rosen, *The New Look of Liberalism.*

introduced as "three guests supreme" Roxanne Roberts, *Opera's Supreme Moment,* WASHINGTON POST, Sept. 8, 2003.

167 *twice-annual opera recitals at the court* Ruth Bader Ginsburg, Remarks for Chautauqua Lawyers in Opera, Jul. 29, 2013.

Chapter 10: But I Just Can't Quit

169 *"Someone who used whatever talent she had"* MSNBC Interview.

"Some of us were angry with her" Justice Ginsburg's Cancer Surgery, THE SITUATION ROOM (CNN television broadcast, Feb. 5, 2009).

170 *"I wanted people to see that the Supreme Court"* Joan Biskupic, *Ginsburg Back with Grit, Grace,* USA TODAY, Mar. 6, 2009.

"I've got a soft spot for Justice Ginsburg" Toobin, *Heavyweight.*

"There was a rapport" Greg Stohr and Matthew Winkler, *Ruth Bader Ginsburg Thinks Americans Are Ready for Gay Marriage,* BLOOMBERG (Feb. 12, 2015).

"It is as though a special, zestful spice" Al Kamen, *Next Year, the Award for Humility,* WASHINGTON POST, May 9, 2001.

"acclaim for your work ethic" Robert Barnes, *Ginsburg Gives No Hint of Giving Up the Bench,* WASHINGTON POST, Apr. 12, 2009.

"it is probable that the female Thurgood Marshall" Randall Kennedy, *The Case for Early Retirement,* NEW REPUBLIC, Apr. 28, 2011.

171 *"she is a complete unique and wonderful gem"* Interview by Shana Knizhnik with Sylvia Law.

"There will be a president after this one" Adam Liptak, *Court Is "One of the Most Activist," Ginsburg Says, Vowing to Stay,* NEW YORK TIMES, Aug. 24, 2013.

"Well, I'm very hopeful about 2016" 92Y Plus, *Ruth Bader Ginsburg and Dorit Beinisch with Nina Totenberg,* YOUTUBE.COM (Oct. 22, 2014).

"and wouldn't that be fantastic" Richard Wolf, *Ginsburg's Dedication Undimmed After 20 Years on Court,* USA TODAY, Aug. 1, 2013.

"When I forget the names of cases" Justice Ginsburg Speaks: Women and the Law; Syria, Congress and the

President and More, THE TAKEAWAY WITH JOHN HOCKENBERRY (Sept. 16, 2013).

172 *Marty's kitchen* Interview by Shana Knizhnik with Anita Fial.

"Sometimes she'll be going to sleep" Interview by Irin Carmon with Jane Ginsburg.

"now there's no one telling me" Beth Saulnier, *Justice Prevails: A Conversation with Ruth Bader Ginsburg '54*, CORNELL ALUMNI MAGAZINE, Nov./Dec. 2013.

"She lives off coffee" Interview by Shana Knizhnik with Clara Spera.

"seek ever more the joys of being alive" Lewis H. Lapham, *Old Masters at the Top of Their Game*, NEW YORK TIMES MAGAZINE, Oct. 23, 2014.

173 *"She asked the marshal if she could"* Interview by Shana Knizhnik with Paul Spera.

"There was a change in the institution" Oral Argument at 07:58, *Obergefell v. Hodges* (No. 14-556).

175 *Under his button-down* Interview by Irin Carmon with Dan Canon.

opinion striking down bans on same-sex marriage Obergefell v. Hodges, 576 U.S. (2015).

RBG's image, rendered in rainbow darth!™, TWITTER (June 26, 2015, 8:41 AM), https:// twitter.com/darth/status/614458561264021504.

Affordable Care Act King v. Burwell, 576 U.S. (2015).

Fair Housing Act Texas Dep't of Hous. and Cmty. Affairs v. Inclusive Cmtys. Project, Inc., 576 U.S. (2015).

Pregnancy Discrimination Act Young v. United Parcel Service, 575 U.S. (2015).

RBG was credited E.g., Adam Liptak, *Right Divided, a Disciplined Left Steered the Supreme Court*, NEW YORK TIMES, June 30, 2015.

175 *"We will never see a day"* MSNBC Interview.

176 *"I passed a door this morning"* Symposium Honoring the 40th Anniversary of Justice Ruth Bader Ginsburg Joining the Columbia Law Faculty: A Conversation with Justice Ginsburg, COLUMBIA LAW SCHOOL (Feb. 10, 2012).

"I think gender discrimination" Exclusive: Ruth Bader Ginsburg on Hobby Lobby, Roe v. Wade, Retirement and Notorious R.B.G., YAHOO NEWS VIDEO (Jul. 31, 2014).

Appendix: How to Be Like RBG

179 *"apathy, selfishness, or anxiety"* Ruth Bader Ginsburg, *Remarks for American Bar Association Initiative: Renaissance of Idealism in the Legal Profession*, May 2, 2006.

"This wonderful woman" Nadine Epstein, *Ruth Bader Ginsburg: "The Notorious RBG,"* MOMENT MAGAZINE, May 2015.

"Fight for the things" Stephanie Garlock, *Ginsburg Discusses Justice and Advocacy at Radcliffe Day Celebration*, HARVARD MAGAZINE, May 29, 2015.

180 *"women belong in all places"* Joan Biskupic, *Ginsburg: Court Needs Another Woman*, USA TODAY, Oct. 5, 2009.

"To stay uncorrupted, the argument goes" Ruth Bader Ginsburg, *Women at the Bar—A Generation of Change*, 2 U. PUGET SOUND LAW REVIEW 1, 12 (1978).

"If you really want to study the law" Conversation with Justice Ruth Bader Ginsburg and Wendy Webster Williams, C-SPAN (Apr. 10, 2009).

181 *"never in it to be the only one"* Interview by Shana Knizhnik with Marcia Greenberger.

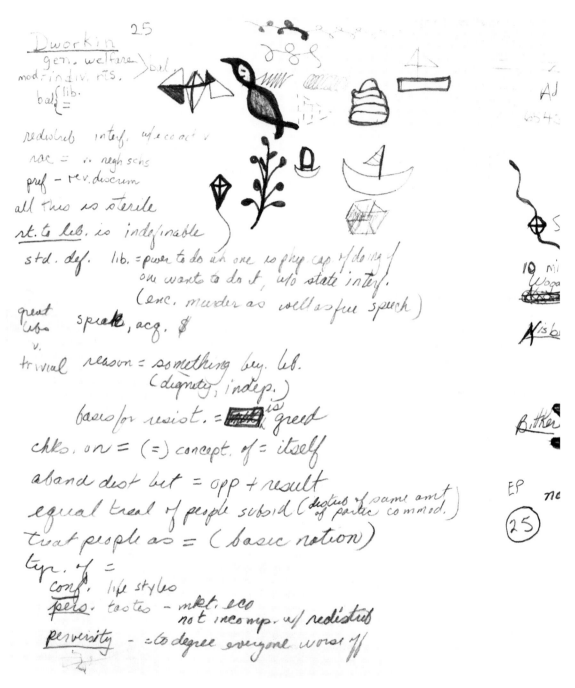

Dworkin 25
  gen. welfare) bal
mod = indiv. rts.
  bal { lib.
        =

redistrib intef. w/ eco act v
rac = v. negh schs
pref - rev. discrim
all this is sterile
rt. to lib. is indefinable
  std. def. lib. = power to do wh one is phys. cap. of doing if
            one wants to do it, w/o state interf.
         (enc. murder as well as free speech)
great
libs   speak, acq. $
  v.
trivial reason = something bey. lib.
        (dignity, indep.)
    basis for resist. = ▮▮▮ is greed
chks. on = (=) concept. of = itself
aband dest but = opp + result
equal treat of people subsid (dictus of same amt
                 of partic commod.)
treat people as = (basic notion)
typ. of =
  conf. life styles
  pers. tastes - mkt. eco
      not incomp. w/ redistrib
  perversity - = to degree everyone worse off

AJ
65 43

10 mi
Woga

A is b

Bitker

EP   no
(25)

RBG's doodles at the Second Circuit Judicial Conference in 1976

Image Credits

Chapter 2: Been in This Game for Years

15   1885 Supreme Court illustration   Library of Congress Prints and Photographs Division/Joseph Ferdinand Keppler

     Sarah Moore Grimké portrait   Library of Congress Prints and Photographs Division

16   Celia Bader photograph   Collection of the Supreme Court of the United States

     Suffrage parade   American Press Association

     Early childhood photograph of Ruth Bader (August 2, 1935)   Collection of the Supreme Court of the United States

     Young Ruth and cousin Richard Bader   Collection of the Supreme Court of the United States

     Lucille Lomen   © Bettmann/CORBIS

     Ruth Bader portrait as Cornell senior (December 1953)   Collection of the Supreme Court of the United States

17   Harvard Law School's 1958 yearbook   Historical and Special Collections, Harvard Law School Library

     Columbia Law Schools' 1959 yearbook   Columbia Law School

     Women on Juries? (1910)   *Harper's Weekly*

     Rutgers School of Law–Newark 1964 yearbook   Rutgers School of Law–Newark

18   JFK signing the Equal Pay Act   Abbie Rowe White House Photographs/John F. Kennedy Presidential Library and Museum, Boston

     LBJ signing Civil Rights Act with MLK, Jr.   Hulton Archive Getty Images

     Estelle Griswold, 1963   Lee Lockwood/The *LIFE* Images Collection/Getty Images

     LBJ and Thurgood Marshall, 1967   Keystone Getty Images

     Flo Kennedy, 1976   Barbara Alper/Getty Images

19   Professor Ginsburg, Columbia Law School   Collection of the Supreme Court of the United States

     Women's protest signs, 1970   Fred W. McDarrah/Getty Images

     Male feminist protester, 1974   Barbara Freeman Getty Images

     Sex Discrimination Casebook   West Publishing Co.

20   Formal portrait of Judge Ruth Bader Ginsburg (fall 1980)   Collection of the Supreme Court of the United States

     Nominee Sandra Day O'Connor and Ronald Reagan   Keystone/CNP/Getty Images

     RBG alone in front of SCOTUS, 1993   Getty Images/Diana Walker

21   State of the Union hug with Barack Obama, 2015   AP Photo/Mandel Ngan, Pool

Chapter 5: Don't Let 'Em Hold You Down

Chapter 6: Real Love

Appendix

Acknowledgments

Notes

Index

Note: *Italicized* page locators indicate images.